What r

MW01678493

A one-of-kind read. Readers learn the thoughts and views of a person with a rich and deep intellect. You will be talking back to her...

—Pam Gross, Beaverton, OR

Reading these miniatures was like having permission to reach into a cookie jar...always a pleasant surprise.

—Robert Buckley, Livermore CA

I loved it!

—Jody Everts, Portland, OR & Helena, MT

If I were teaching women's history, I would have it as required reading. It represents an American woman's experiences in the mid to late 20th century and into our current one. You do not diminish or exaggerate your roles. Thank you for sharing your experiences in such an appealing manner.

—Cynthia Bertsch, Sheboygan, WI

This inspired retrospective delves deeply into the soul of a modern woman who found her way forward by trusting her roots to guide her. While not a continuous narrative in an autobiographical sense, it nevertheless leads readers to reflect on their own encounters with the spirit and struggles of their times.

—Gerry Bertsch, Sheboygan, WI

Also by Sally Petersen

Remembrances: Class of 1950,
Holdrege High School
(limited edition)

The Real American Dream: Creating Independence
and Running a One-Person Business

Miniatures
(chapbook)

Tea Pie, Love and Reality:
A Collection of Memoir Essays

I May Never Get to Petra

a second collection of memoir essays

Sally Petersen

First Edition

ISBN: 978-0-9791559-7-0

Cover art: "Color Splash" by Jody Everts
Cover and book design: Anita Jones, Another Jones Graphics

Publisher's Cataloging-In-Publication Data

Names: Petersen, Sally R., author.
Title: I may never get to Petra : a second collection of memoir essays / Sally Petersen.
Other titles: Tea pie, love and reality.
Description: First edition. | Portland, OR : Petersen Publications, [2017] | Further brief essays following the author's "Tea, pie, love and reality" (c2010).
Identifiers: ISBN: 978-0-9791559-7-0 | LCCN: 2017934259
Subjects: LCSH: Petersen, Sally R. | Life. | Self-realization. | Family. | Nature. | Spirituality. | Attitude (Psychology) | LCGFT: Essays. | Autobiographies.
Classification: LCC: CT275.P5843 P482 2017 | DDC: 920/.073--dc23

PetersenPublications.com
SallyPetersen.com

Contents

Introduction

Here, the reliable eyewitness!

The classroom door flies open. A person steps into the room and fires a small handgun. The professor falls, clutching his chest, as the gunman turns and races out, slamming the door behind him.

Before stunned students can react, the professor is on his feet. "Tell me what you saw," he commands his students. "Describe it."

Students will report one shot fired, or two, or several. They will have the man wearing a mask or glasses, he'll be tall or short, red-haired or blonde, white or brown, he will—or won't—have spoken or gestured. He may even be described as a woman in man's clothing.

Journalists, and others, will recognize this classic exercise designed to show that eyewitnesses are unreliable, that no two people see and remember the same way even immediately after an event.

We see differently, therefore we remember differently. We interpret and draw conclusions based on memory, on what we thought we saw.

If we understand this, if we stop trying to claim scientific accuracy or religious authority for our personal observations and conclusions, to me that would be wonderful, simply utopian. Much could be smoothed out in life if we own our responses while recognizing that others will not respond the same way because they see and think differently.

So here, then. I offer you bits and pieces of how I've looked at life, the world around me, people, things and situations. I don't vouch for their technical accuracy, but I do own them.

Although I live in and love the West Coast, at heart you have here a Nebraskan with a straight-ahead gaze and a practical attitude. I believe in possibilities as one might who grew up surrounded by the infinite space and endless skies of the Great Plains.

The Plains and their history also taught that disaster can appear unexpectedly—ferocious early spring snowstorms, inch-thick ice covering the world while stopping travel and electricity, Biblical plagues of grasshoppers, gully-washer rains that overwhelm the earth, tornados. So I take nothing for granted.

I see myself as Everywoman, confronted with the common joys and fears of family, of making my way in a man's world, of deciding my next course in life, interested in travel, nature, and writing.

Sometimes I see my life as a series of rooms filled with a tangled, more or less random conglomeration of activities, places, people, thoughts, feelings, reactions, learning and the occasional gem. I write about these things in a short form I call Miniatures.

Each miniature is a peek into one of my rooms, into what I observed or felt at the time. These are rooms we may share—travel, work, living with nature, family, moving. The miniature won't tell you everything about my room, but it may set you to thinking. You might have reacted differently, or maybe not. Either way, the dialogue begins…

It took several years until I finally got downsizing right. First my husband Jim and I moved out of a big house/ big yard into a retirement home duplex. Then we rented a great apartment with a view on the Oregon Coast, intending to stay six months or so. After two and a half years, we moved back to urban living in a condo close to downtown Portland.

It all began with a garage sale.

The garage sale

They are like archaeologists sifting in desert ruins for the one artifact that will justify their trip—a pottery shard, a bronze coin bearing a ruler's profile, a saber tooth in the remains of a cooking fire.

Or like drifters in Filene's basement picking through clothing piles for the right acid-green blouse to embolden a charcoal-brown suit, for expensive shoes that fit, for a cashmere sweater to top chinos.

Or like doctoral students combing through museum drawers with white-gloved fingers or searching papyrus pages for the arcane figure or fact they know will bolster a thesis topic.

Or like French country women at the outdoor market, checking to see which fish have clear eyes, which cheese has the proper aroma, which daisies are freshest.

The morning hopefuls arrive early. Some excavate for the small rocking chair, or shyly finger the iridescent salmon-pink prom dress.

A neighbor returns to snap up two stepladders at day's end mark-down prices.

A last-minute wanderer tucks an Irish fishing hat and a 1970s pink plaid beret under her arm while plunking a blue sunshade on her grey curls.

"I'll take them all," she announces boldly. "I'm Grandma Cookie! I used to have a hundred and fifty hats!"

—*May 7-8, 2010*

What to keep-1

When you have all the space in the world, a fourteen-foot kitchen island surrounded by storage space, master suite with walk-in closet, bathroom and a dressing room, two-room office and a guest room filled with your mother's mahogany furniture, you don't have to make decisions about what to buy, what to keep, what to display. You *can* have it all.

But when you're shoehorned into a small space, and your furniture hasn't shrunk, decisions must be made.

My favorite was a small decision. I put an efficient slick business card holder in the Goodwill box while deciding to keep my cards in the old amethyst-encrusted brass box.

—*September 2013*

What to keep-2

I keep the seashells, handled over the years and admired by grandchildren, for their beauty, like the angel wing, or their stories, like the chambered nautilus, or their oddity, like the brain coral.

Rocks? Because the black obsidian shines on one side and you can see how it could be chipped for toolmaking. The Biggs rocks show pictures of mountains when they're sliced, and thunder eggs have beautiful crystal worlds inside—or not. My father found the three-pound amethyst geode in the hills above Arch Cape.

The glowing green glass Japanese fishing floats? Because they traveled the circumference of the Pacific Ocean, perhaps several times, before my dad or I washed off the barnacles and brought them home (our collections now merged).

Fossils? Because the trilobites populated oceans that no longer exist, the inch and a half long fish once swam in Wyoming, the shark's tooth menaces from its surrounding rock.

I love these things. I'll keep three rocks, four fossils, six shells and one of every size fishing float to represent the rest as I trim down for my next journey.

If it's nature that nurtures me, why then do I keep the silly four-inch enameled teapot with cats on it?

Because it makes me smile.

—2010

Four o'clock on a rainy afternoon

What am I going to do with the wedding photos and albums? How did I end up with so many?

Here sit two white leather albums from my first wedding. One is mine, of course, the other could be from my former spouse's parents. Or my parents, all of them gone now. Have you noticed that all weddings from the 1950s look alike?

Here's my oldest daughter's first wedding. Instead of an album, dozens of color snapshots that amount to the same thing. Mementos of a nasty marriage. My mother looking gray and exhausted after a plane trip across the country, here the long, faux-country flowered dresses of the early seventies worn by all the daughters and half the guests. Memories of how the bridegroom's friends snuck out of the reception at our house with unopened bottles of champagne under their coats.

Here's another album. The second daughter. We held that wedding at a small church on the California coast. It was fun: friends came from far places, and a young minister who'd been a great friend officiated. But the groom was a cipher and his family a small, unsociable unit. The brief marriage caused only a tiny blip in my daughter's life, a smaller one in mine, except for the memory of a good party.

The next daughter's wedding to the biggest ego ever to leave New York City also filled a pretty venue on the California coast. I seemed to be the only family member who liked the bridegroom's parents. Since technically this is a step-daughter, and technicalities seem to run weddings, I had no place in the proceedings. She tried to include me, bless her heart. But I not only felt awkward, but in every photo I look awkward. She gleamed with beauty, but the union didn't survive. The wedding album, a gift from his mother, did though.

Finally, a mixture of opposites highlights the fourth daughter's album. She chose the site of the ceremony, a high alpine meadow in the Rockies. She wears my first wedding dress, her attendants are two black labs with blue flower collars and the bridegroom is stunning. He chose the reception site, an elegant old hotel in Boulder, the highest-priced venue around. Their differences continued. She hiked, skied or ran outdoors; he used a gym and played handball inside walls. He sought groups; she preferred a fire and a good book. She gardened, he bought a red Harley. The marriage didn't last.

So, there they are, lovely photos, formal and informal, from five weddings.

Is there a moral to this story? I think not.

So I'm going to pour a glass of wine, put the photos and albums in a box, label it "Weddings that didn't last" and deliver it to the garage. Someone else can deal with it another time.

—November, 2010

Preserved in Amber

Why do certain pieces of clothing demand to be kept?

Is it memory? Maybe I can't bear to lose the occasions on which I wore them, the part of my life surrounding each article?

Perhaps the appeal of the article itself? The subtle contrast of shining red silk with the classic design of a shirtwaist? Or the patterned, thick-textured black and red wrap-around skirt with a simple black, long sleeved, boat neck top? I've kept the gown an artist friend said looks like a Monet painting. Again the contrast I seem to like—a complex print of bright blue, soft pinks and washed watercolors with simple construction, so the eye sees mainly the swirl of color, the tiny waist.

Are these dresses domestic versions of amber-encased beetles that contain both information and beauty?

—1998

Adventure (Day One)

Turns out that a retirement community wasn't right for us, even a lovely one, filled with people we'd come to care for. So two life-long dreams presented themselves as alternatives: living in the south of France or the Oregon Coast. We chose the easier option.

On Thursday, Sept. 6, movers packed belongings from our duplex at the Portland retirement community; Friday we met them at the coastal apartment at nine a.m. They were the two Mexican kids who'd packed and unpacked us twice, making them practically old friends. On a quick lunch break, one trotted down one hundred and seventy-four steps to put his feet in the ocean he'd never seen. The other tried to get us to adopt him ("I don't eat much," he said with a grin. "And I'm no trouble at all."). They finished unloading mid-afternoon and we said we'd see them when we moved back to Portland in a year.

Jim and I collapsed into the deck chairs, opened a bottle of prosecco and luxuriated in the windless, sunny warmth. Gray whales spouted from the kelp bed in the Pacific below us. We know the sparkling blue sea and blazing sunsets won't last long. Soon it will be as if someone turned a fire hose on our ocean-facing windows and our world will turn grey for days, maybe weeks on end. We're ready.

Jim said, "Remember, we're on vacation." We're not, of course, but we plan to reclaim that carefree feeling.

After downing the bottle of bubbly with cheese and crackers, we made up the bed, unpacked a bit and slept the sleep of the just.

—September 7, 2012

Downsizing 101

Just before we moved, Architectural Digest ran an article about a designer and his partner who live in a seven hundred and thirty-two square foot apartment in New York City. To make it sound glamorous they asked, "Why not live in the ultimate hotel suite?" In the fine print, we learned this is not their only home and she keeps a lot of her clothing in the other place. But it did remind us that space isn't everything.

A friend told us about people who had moved three separate families into a very small home. "How did you decide what to keep?" she asked, aghast at the thought.

"We each decided to keep only what we absolutely love. That way we are surrounded with things we love in each room."

Good idea, we thought, for starters. But we love everything we own, having disposed of borderline items long before this move. So here are our "move and downsize rules," devised on the spot.

- Reduce multiples (six wine glasses, not twenty, one or two large bowls instead of six, one presentation platter only).
- Make the basic food-serving unit two, not twelve-plus.
- Substitute a small bar-height table with two chairs for the Duncan Phyfe that would seat twenty.

- Re-think placement and use of furnishings. (Move the Korean chest that once held holiday china and silver to the kitchen for daily plates, bowls and serving dishes.)
- Don't unpack anything you won't use in a year. Place two red dots on a box to mean: "We won't need anything here until the next move."
- Repack if you violate the rule above.
- Repack to consolidate boxes. Then re-label when contents of boxes change.
- Don't be merely practical: (Display the fishing floats and some art glass, one or two paintings.)
- Reduce clutter, it is the enemy of small places. (Fewer pictures on walls; fewer books in cases; fewer things sitting around.)
- Exchange large vases for ones that will take a small bouquet or a bloom or two; keep fresh flowers year-round.
- Buy a few items designed for small houses. (Hanging shampoo and soap holders for showers, small kitchen counter unit to hold dishcloth, scrubbers, brushes.)

This will be like backpacking: If we don't have it, we'll do without or improvise field expedients.

—*September 2012*

Like ratty old shawls (Day Two)

The resident gray whales breech and blow at 6:30 p.m. (They would do this every three or four days, as if they knew we were on the deck waiting for them, sipping Finlaggan with our smoked cheese and garlic-stuffed green olives.) No doubt they'd sent spires of white foam into the blue air in other autumns, but we didn't see.

We'd made our second move within a year, leaving family, good friends, and a sure-bet life in the city for a beach rental and an unknown future.

By definition all future is unknown, isn't it? So we acknowledge it, deciding to let the future care for itself, begin to live in the present.

We slip chronological age from our shoulders like ratty old shawls. Those shoulders then drop to their rightful places from the stiff, hunched positions they'd assumed under the weight of expectations.

We watch the sunset, waiting for the rare miracle of the green flash. If it happens, we'll be there to see.

—September 2012

Centered (Day Three)

It's a soft night, our third in the beach house. Out the great window that fronts the ocean, a point of white light from a fishing boat glows on the horizon, marking the midway point between dark sea and dark sky.

Like a diamond in a navel, I think, dividing a body with a gleam of beauty.

—September 2012

Why indeed? (Day Four)

So, tell me please, why do I continue to unpack cut glass bowls, crystal goblets and porcelain teacups way into the evening on the fourth night? Why do I line them up precisely, taking such pleasure in their gleam on the shelves of the Danish teak hutch?

Gleam, glow, twinkle, shine, flash, sparkle, glimmer, shimmer…I love the words associated with shiny objects. I love the objects, too. I'm not yet ready to give them up.

And I *do* know why I unpacked them; they belong on that shelf. They stand there, ready for use.

The next morning on Day Five, reality intrudes, as it has a way of doing. I retrieve the box and bubble wrap, begin to re-pack. The beach life we intend does not include candlelit dinners for twelve, damask cloths and wine from crystal decanters.

—September 2012

Floats (Day Five)

The green glass fishing floats, plus one brown and a small purple float, drifted their way around the Pacific Ocean nearly sixty years ago. Since then they've been with me in seven homes in three states.

Today I place them on the deck high above the water not far from where I found the biggest ones rolling in on a late afternoon tide. My father used a driftwood stick to locate the smaller ones in foam left by winter storms on the Arch Cape beach.

—September 2012

Light bulbs (Day 6)

I change out the six round bulbs above the sink for blue "natural spectrum" ones. They're less harsh bouncing off the white walls of the bathroom in our beach rental. I look better.

Although I believe I should put myself together each morning in the glaring reality of light bulb honesty, I won't. I've opted for a softer, friendlier version of reality.

—September 2012

A trade (Day 7)

We've traded city sophistication for Oregon beach casual. This means jeans, fleece toppers and boots. Not cute little stiletto-heeled boots, either. These boots have Gore-Tex uppers for the rain and lug soles for traction in sand.

—September 2012

It's not the toy, it's the child (Third week)

As I walk around the elevated track at the community center, pre-schoolers play in the gym below me.

The girl-child is golden-haired and delicate. She's playing with a little plastic grocery cart.

The boy-child is sturdy, purposeful in his walk. He's playing with a plastic gas pump, complete with attached hose and nozzle.

She leans over, straightens her arms in front of her and rams the grocery cart across the gym at full speed like an angel of destruction, crashing into the protective padding at the far end with glee and great sounds.

He slings the hose and nozzle over his shoulder and sashays with the gas pump as if it were his mother's purse.

—Lincoln City, 2013

Pecking orders (Fourth week)

The African night fell and in Etosha Park rangers turned on the lights, illuminating a big water hole. Travelers watched from benches as the evening show began. Dainty springbok appeared first. They tactfully shared their space for a while when the giraffes came by. Since the latter knelt to drink, they sipped in small groups with some always on the lookout. Finished, they ambled away into darkness.

The sociable zebras arrived in herds, jostling, drinking quickly and leaving. They were accompanied by an occasional gemsbok. Other larger antelopes of the park showed up wearing their impossibly lovely horns: the kudu, the oryx.

As they left, some of the more dangerous creatures began to appear, the ugly ones. Hyenas and warthogs.

Then the waterhole cleared completely and into silence stepped the lions, loosely arranged into their prides: mothers, cubs, and the kings, keeping a respectful distance from one another. They drank their fill, leaving when the rhinoceroses showed up, smaller ones first, then the two-thousand pound tanks.

Two of the big male rhinos trotted away from the rest and began a loud argument. They roared, grunted, stomped and rushed at each other, stopping nose to nose, for fifteen or twenty minutes. Noise filled the night and the ground shook. All but the irritable fighters had drifted away when the atmosphere changed.

The enormous dark grey shapes slowly materializing from the darker grey background looked unstoppable. The elephants were led in a slow-moving single file by maybe four thousand pounds of trunk-swinging matriarch. Babies and families followed her into the water. The little ones played with the frantic energy of youngsters out after bedtime, while mothers and aunties drank and bathed with their trunks. They took all the time they wanted before moving on to blend again into the night.

After this domestic scene the real kings appeared. Teen-age male elephants arrived in buddy-like pairs, the elders came alone. Their great size diminished the world around them. Together but separately they drank and bathed with ponderous elegance before leaving the water to settle back into clearness. The next creatures would not show until dawn.

I thought of hierarchies, as another version unfolded below me in the gym one morning.

Below me two rangy dads with basketball bodies helped their three- or four-year-old sons get the idea of the game. Neither youngster was strong enough to throw a ball all the way to the basket, so the dads hoisted them up.

In the gym door came five older boys, probably seventh-graders.

Inevitably the older kids and the dads gravitated to each other. For a few minutes they shot hoops, ran and guarded, took the measure of each other's skills. Next they formed a game with one dad and two younger players on each side with the extra kid rotating from the bench.

While the bigger, stronger males indulged their prowess, off to one side of the gym the little ones, no longer relevant, played together.

—Summer 1993 and Autumn 2013

The broach (Fourth month)

At the coast, our cars sat outside in the salty dampness of the Oregon Coast. They didn't prosper.

Yet, more than once, in the night, dew settled on the side view mirrors. The next morning, sunshine hitting the little droplets turned the passenger-side mirror into a huge pavé diamond broach.

It sparkled under the words, "objects in the mirror are closer than they appear."

—December, 2013

Watching the moon

Some nights the moon shines fluorescent, cold and blue, projecting a silver path on a calm sea.

Some nights the moon glows incandescent, hanging over the dark sea with the lustrous warmth of the lights on the lone fishing boat.

Tonight the shining path on the water is touched with gold.

—Dec. 7, 2013

Turning onto Coast Avenue

Often when I come around the corner and see the beach directly ahead, I notice two people standing close to the surf twined around each other.

They're whip-like young, or chunky middle age, or even-from-a-distance-you-can-tell old.

Something about a warm sun, waves lapping and seagulls twinkling overhead makes lovers of any age want to touch.

—Summer, 2014

People say the most astonishing things. Sometimes we miss them because it's a family member talking.

Chaos and the tree

"A weeping willow would look nice by your pond," I commented one day, viewing the yard in Memphis.

"I don't want one," says the daughter. "They're scary."

We were interrupted before I could inquire further.

Back home in Oregon, walking by a pond I frequented, for several days I watched closely as a clump of willow trees filled out with spring energy.

Scary?

Then I saw it. These tall trees resemble the waterfall illustration in James Gleick's *Chaos* book. Remember it? Water begins its plunge in discreet packets, and disintegrates into non-recurring, random sprays on the way down.

Order descending into chaos. Yes, scary.

I wonder if that's what she saw, or if she was responding to a frightening childhood memory or imagination.

I'll ask sometime.

—July 2009

The day before Thanksgiving

"Well," the grandmother smiled to her hostess-in-training, "the first thing is to decide whether the tablecloth needs ironing."

Grandkids had arrived the day before Thanksgiving, to help set the table. It was a custom much favored by the grandmother who hoped to transmit down the generations her joy in a table well set with porcelain, gleaming sterling and crystal goblets set on damask.

Together they decided yes, the creamy cloth was wrinkled.

The twelve-year-old granddaughter had become something of a history buff. She knew more about the heavy black irons her great-grandmothers heated on the back of wood stoves than about a modern steam iron.

So the lesson began: how to set up the ironing board, which side to stand on and why. How to plug in the iron, fill it, and set the heat range for linen. They discussed how the combination of heat and steam made life easy—especially compared with the black iron antiques they took from a nearby shelf and compared to the gleaming Sunbeam.

Shining black hair swung as the child leaned to her task. The large cloth arranged just so, the learner swept the hot tool grandly over and back, picking up the motion with ease. She moved the cloth, gave adjacent wrinkles her steam-and-heat treatment. Another section smoothed out, then another.

Suddenly the iron stopped moving and her head came up sharply, eyes big:

"Oh! Now I know why people iron! Things look better!"

She went on to iron a dozen gigantic linen napkins and by the time she had finished was trying to get the purple tee shirt off her younger sister so she could make it look better too.

—December 2010

Nothing spicy for me, please

Clearing out boxes of old papers, books and miscellany, I find a sheet of lined writing paper with Mickey Mouse in the lower right corner. A daughter's name is on it.

The Mexican food is hot
My parents say it is not
I don't like it
My sister likes it a bit
I don't care for it
But I guess I could
if I should

This daughter is now in her mid-forties and still regards catsup as one of the spicy foods.

—2005

Out of the mouth of babes…

My daughter sat on my lap in the pink rocking chair for her afternoon story, our favorite time of the day. Her warm little body eased against me as I wrapped my arms around her and began a new book, *Winnie The Pooh.*

The idyll didn't last long. First she began to wiggle, then she tossed off the lap blanket. She began chattering, distracting me. I couldn't read. Something going on here.

"What's wrong, honey?"

"I don't like that little bear."

—Fall, 1963

The animal child

Gardening on terraces by the Des Moines house, the three-year-old blonde found them—maybe an inch long, sightless, hairless, abandoned. Mouse babies, four of them.

At her insistence, we emptied a matchbox, filled it with cotton, located an eye dropper and moved into rescue mode. When they were old enough, we released them.

She acquired subsequent animals over the years. All were bigger than that first lot—a huge tiger cat, a black teacup poodle, a rat, white mice, hamsters and guinea pigs. Birds joined the menagerie from time to time—finches, a parakeet. Eventually she had a horse, a feisty pinto with wanderlust. We chased that horse around many suburban cul de sacs near her stable.

Early on, life brought this child to the West Coast. Eventually she acquired four children, acreage, and a husband who wanted Boston terriers. Today she presides over two Bostons, an ever-changing assemblage of cats and exotic chickens the children show at the county fair.

And hogs. Three hundred and fifty pound Durocs bring county and state fair ribbons to the children who show them. And a smile to the face of the woman who began with inch-long mouse babies a half-continent away.

—2016

The recent graduate

At the West Linn Italian restaurant: "I've never had lamb before. I'll try that."

At a Lihue food cart: "I've never eaten Thai before. I'll try that."

At Japanese Kintaro in Kapa'a: "Sure, I'll try the sashimi."

He's all in, this kid.

—Summer, 2015

Uses of avoidance

Here's my favorite example of what you can do with avoidance.

My parents were visiting us in the Pacific Northwest when Dad learned his youngest brother was fast losing his life to cancer. It would have been easy to detour into the Bay Area for a final visit on his way back home to Nebraska.

When Mom and I suggested it, Dad didn't want to go.

"Glen is so ill he might not want to see anyone."

He died a month later. Dad didn't want to travel "all the way out to California when Glen wouldn't know it anyway."

So he didn't go when he was dying, then he didn't go because he was dead.

Like all good avoiders, he also had a backup reason for not making either trip; he didn't much like Glen's wife!

Avoidance gets bad press but it handles some things really well.

It can spare you when *at that time* confronting or dealing with circumstances would be more damaging to you than letting them drift by. I suspect this was operating for my father.

It can serve as protection when you don't have the right skills for dealing with a situation.

Avoidance can cool off a tricky situation, allowing you to deal with it later, quietly. Some can't-win situations are best avoided forever.

But if it's your only, or even primary, method of dealing with issues, avoidance can lead to depression and increased anxiety. It's a tool for coping with life, nothing more. Like all tools, it can be used wisely or badly.

If you use avoidance, be aware of what you're doing; choose it deliberately. Make avoidance another string in your bow, not the only one.

—1959-2009

What would I tell children about life?

Be brave and have fun.

—June, 1016

Zen master

We have a six-foot, three-inch Zen master staying temporarily in our downstairs room. This twenty-four-year old Zenster wears no robes. Being colorblind, he solves all clothing issues with black jeans and a black hoodie.

He appears silently from below and just as silently leaves. He's polite—always a smile and a "Hi, grandma"—but rarely offers himself. We must approach him with a question or remarks. Then he speaks in brief phrases whose meaning may or may not be clear.

He often is struck with awe. We know this because he solemnly intones "Awesome" in response to many comments.

Like a true master, he experiences the rewards of menial tasks. When asked to mow the lawn or empty the dishwasher, he gravely nods, "No problem."

He dispenses advice just as briefly. This morning, I mentioned a headache. "Drink water."

Every home should have its own Zen master.

—Spring, 2010

Divorce

Divorce doesn't end a relationship, it merely changes it.

—1976

Writers are just like everyone else—except when they're not.

People who write

Writers have blue pen marks on their bed sheets.

Writers buy pens by the box and keep sharpened #2 pencils although they seldom use them.

Writers buy printer paper by the case, and keep backup cartridges just in case a new draft needs to be run out late at night.

Writers with sinus trouble love to iron. The steam clears their heads while the smoothing action brings creative ideas. Never mind that now fabrics are no-iron and wrinkles are cool and the job can be hired out.

Writers often cook things that require chopping, like stir fry or soups or salads with long lists of ingredients. Never mind that you can buy almost everything chopped by someone else. Or go to a restaurant.

Writers who iron and chop frequently pause to write down the ideas that come during the process.

Creativity dotes on small, repetitive actions.

—April 2015

Inspiration

George Balanchine, the dancer and choreographer, said:

"There is no such thing as inspiration. It's not anything that is all of a sudden, like a stomach ache or something. You have to work through certain things—and sweat...you have to know how to cook, for instance. You must know how to put together things…

"We don't create, actually, we assemble what God created. See, it's already there, anyhow. You just choose. You must take what's in front of you, and you manipulate it, put it together."

I scribbled those notes on the back of an envelope, fascinated when I heard them on a PBS broadcast on Balanchine's hundredth birthday anniversary.

A recent article about the famous Balanchine quotes and their sources said that much of his most inspirational thought is directly traceable to others. Apparently he read widely and, like many of us, remembered what he read but not where he read it.

So maybe the words above came from someone else. After all, the idea is hardly new, although his phrases are homey, like stomach ache and the great reference to cooking—"You must know how to put together things."

How much does it matter where your ideas, your notions and inspiration come from?

According to Balanchine, we all "… take what's in front of [us]…put it together…assemble what God created."

That is creativity.

(Notes taken from a PBS "Live from Lincoln Center" broadcast on George Balanchine's 100th Birthday Anniversary, May, 2004)

(The article is maybe from the New Yorker. winter-spring, 2009)

In the California desert

Today I need to be alone the way a thirsty person needs water.

I'm in a city where I know only three people and my gregarious husband is with them somewhere else. I'm grateful.

Wordsworth knew about this, and his short poem floats into memory—the world has been "too much with us; late and soon."

I mutter "and for way too long."

I head to the balcony to write.

As I position the computer Emily Dickinson pops into my mind. Of course. A woman whose life story is a reminder that a rich sensibility doesn't need much external stimulation.

Think about her, I tell myself. *She has come into your mind for a reason.*

Two weeks later, at home, a friend hands me an essay about the French painter Pierre Bonnard. He led an exceptionally ordered life of seclusion, ostensibly to accommodate the desires and needs of the woman he loved. But his self-constrained life surely suited him since he painted with success and apparent contentment for many years.

Think about Bonnard, I tell myself again. *A second lesson has fallen into your hands.*

I sigh.

What a task to create peace. I'm so drawn into the twenty-four-hour news cycle, land lines and cell phones, texting, social networks, email, television, websites, magazines, newspapers. Wordsworth, Dickinson and Bonnard didn't have to put up with that!

Uh-oh. I'm whining. That means it's time to take action.

A belated New Year's resolution emerges: *Remember Dickinson and Bonnard this year.*

—January 2007

Change

Realization crystallized a year ago—I must create change hour by hour, over time, or never.

Never is closer than it used to be.

So I turn my life into calmer seas, creating a life better suited to me. A writer's life, centered on process.

I ignore a duty, forgo a long lunch, don't return every call. Little acts, tiny turns of the wheel, incremental momentum in the turn. The ship turns slowly, making no visible waves.

I finish writing my first book.

—November 2, 1999

Making a tapestry

Can you weave a tapestry with three threads? Can you tell a life with three topics?

How about a work thread, a family thread, a self-awareness thread?

How about adding your interaction with history, changing times, ideas? What about where you lived, the sustenance offered your heart by singing winds and prairie grass, by space itself? Are these subsumed in work, relationships, self?

What color would be the threads, the primary colors of life?

Work is blue: sky, sea, the blue wind, calm, clear, orderly, lacking drama.

Family is yellow: yellow is the color of madness, butter, sun and fun. When yellow is a little off true, it becomes acid and corrodes. All other relationships are part of this thread, so infinite colors of yellow are possible. When work and relationships fuse well, they become green for growth, accomplishment, anticipation. When yellow turns to orange and combines with work it can become brown and desiccated like cow dung on the dust.

Self is red: the flame of passion, of anger. When mixed with white it becomes the cool warmth of pink. Red can be the light saber of suddenly realized truth, the warmth of coals being banked to last the night.

Yes, I think we could write a life, weave a tapestry, with three threads.

—When I first contemplated writing a memoir, 2007

I never would have thought to write about some subjects if they hadn't been assigned as writing prompts. Among them: tell us about the night you were conceived! What an idea!

In writing groups with a leader, the prompt is a common device for jumpstarting creativity. The randomness of the prompt usually brings up fresh ideas. Or it coalesces something we've been ruminating on but haven't brought to the surface.

Responses to writing prompts sometimes are dreadful, but also they can be little gems, attached to nothing but themselves.

The next items were collected from my jewel box of responses to writing prompts. They've been accumulating over the years. All but one came from workshops conduced by an Irish poet who, in response to her own inner prompt, changed her name from Annie Callan to Ana Ramana.

What do I imagine happened the night I was conceived?*

Oh, I think an enormous heavenly cymbal crashed and young angels giggled in anticipation.

I think little pink and white ruffled dresses starched and ironed themselves in sunlit closets and red wagons polished their wheels. I think snows—white, reflective, crystal cold and lovely—piled up in the corner, readying themselves for her first winter. Peonies—rambunctious, burgundy balls of color—tucked up a thousand petals for her first spring.

She would be born on All Saints Day, so throughout the firmament the designated ones met to decide on gifts. They put love, a good mind, stamina, joy and fun in the little picnic basket they prepared for her. They saved their best for last. At the moment when the soon-to-be-child implanted herself firmly where warmth and food existed, she received the greatest gift of all—gratitude.

**Prompt from a meditation: "What do you imagine happened the night you were conceived?"*

—8/09/15

At one time I looked forward...*

At one time I looked forward. No. That's not true. That's not right. At one time I did not look forward, I simply lived.

Kittens tumble and roll, stretch their little paws out for a bauble, fall asleep. Babies grab for an outstretched finger, bite into it. Young people inhale San Francisco, or Florence, or a farm or a city, experience love or lust for the first time. Life bubbles around them, immersing their young bodies in newness.

At one time I was buoyed by that kind of excitement, by learning—oh how I love to learn—by experiencing bits and pieces of life for the first time. I lived fully illuminated by quick flashes of rising joy.

Now, I do look forward. I plan. I analyze. I'm thoughtful, careful, grown up.

How I miss them, those lovely, long years of firsts.

**Prompt from a poem: "at one time I looked forward..."*

A predictable little essay*

So what could, would, should, might, I have done differently in my life?

How much time do you have to listen? Hours? Days? Years?

I'm old, Child, with a lifetime of small acts of rudeness that remain in my memory to be regretted at leisure. A lifetime of failures-to-act that follow me to bed when the lights go out. A lifetime of half-baked ideas, of projects begun but not completed, of lofty goals naively articulated without understanding yet that I lack the single-mindedness to reach them.

Lots of things could have been done differently—but then this life would not have been mine, would it? I'd have been a different person if at each, or really any, decision point I'd gone another way. I might have been more loving, or accomplished, or I might have reared my girl children better. I might not have divorced Ken or married Jim, or joined the corporate world for a while or gained an extra twenty pounds, or...or...or...

But the sun shines warm today and a small breeze ruffles the red rhododendron blossoms outside the open door. I'm surrounded by old friends and possible new ones. I didn't forget my lunch. Life—ahhh, it's good. I'll worry another day about the roads I didn't take. Today, I'll enjoy the ones I did.

**Prompt from a poem: "What would you have done differently?"*

—May 31, 2015

I dream…*

I dream of being svelte.

Such a fine word, svelte, so evocative of a lovely being.

The svelte woman embodies the idea of slender, of sophistication, of no excess subcutaneous fat. Embodies the idea of slipping smoothly through life, perfectly poised for each instant, not braced but briefly balanced for activity.

Svelte.

Sveetie, you should be so lucky!

—April 23, 2007

Best read aloud

**Prompt: what do you dream of?*

I buried my…*

Once, long ago, I buried my dreams in the bustle of life. Now they have reappeared, refreshed and strengthened by their long underground stay.

"Dreams die," they say.

"Not mine," I reply.

I buried my joy when I learned to attend to life's mundane details. I became efficient, effective, disciplined. I can create order from pandemonium, wrestle chaos itself to a standstill.

It's time to reach again for joy.

I want it back.

I buried my hands in the warmth of yours.

Since then, I have not let go.

**Prompt from a poem: "I buried my…"*

Most mornings*

I want to meet the girl who saw mighty possibilities before her, who knew there would be more to her world than safety and stability and "Would you change the lightbulb, dear?" And "It's time to do the laundry." And "Shall we have the New Year's Eve party again?"

I want to meet the girl who knew one husband would not be enough, two children not enough, one locale not enough. Who understood more and sought it. Who reached beyond her grasp.

When she did, when unhappiness, discontent and restlessness visited her, she treated these visitors as temporary, as messengers, as spurs to change.

She didn't always run her country, but often enough.

When I greet her in the mirror most mornings I am happy for her.

**After "I Want to Meet the Girl" by Naomi Nye*

—2010

My inner child...*

My inner child is petulant.
She says, "Can't," "Won't."

She sits on the back step in the sun and watches ants crawling around the crack in the back yard sidewalk, going places.

She wonders what it would be like to be one of them with a real job to do: No questions asked, Miss Ant, up and over, in and out, back to the beginning, then do it again.

She thinks she might like that. Then she says, "Won't go."

My inner child is tired of figuring things out. She pouts and says, "Don't know."

My inner child is two years old, learning to say no.

Sometimes my outer child lets her have her way… "no," "don't know," "won't go," "can't," "won't." Those are peaceful days…a book read, a nap taken, a child indulged.

**Prompt: "It's a cliché, your inner child, but see what you can do with it."*

—08/09/15

Promises*

Promises made, promises kept, promises broken.

Promises to following generations: "Your people can fish here at Celilo as long as the sun rises and sets."

Promises made with the best of intentions: "I will love you forever."

Those made of desperation, when everything is gone but words, and words can instill hope: "Of course Santa will bring the doll you want."

Ugly promises: a cruel person who vowed to create such pressure in my daughter's life that her cancer would "come back and kill her."

Beautiful promises, whether believed or not: "I go to prepare a room for you" or "We'll meet on the other side some day," or "It won't hurt."

Implicit promises: "I've given birth to you and I will protect and cherish you."

Public promises: "Until death do us part," or "I will honor my vows."

Private promises: "I'll walk every day, finish the manuscript by fall, take care of myself."

Harmless promises: "You'll enjoy this show," "It's not too spicy," "Only take a minute," "Be right there."

We live by them and die by them. Promises made, promises kept, promises broken.

**Obviously this prompt had to do with promises…*

The muse*

Y'know, I always have trouble with personifying ideas. Like when they turn God into an old guy with a white beard who sits on a throne. Or make a muse into a Greek maiden with diaphanous draperies. Or a sexy woman in a tight red dress and piled up black hair.

(By the way, why isn't the muse ever a tall blonde guy in tight jeans, a checked flannel shirt and scuffed hiking boots?)

My muse isn't a person. It's an idea that often comes at an awkward time. It's the product, I'd guess, of some neurons firing in a brain that's busy working on another subject. Or trying to go to sleep. Or engaged in conversation. Or driving on a busy street where stopping to take notes wouldn't work.

Maybe that's why we personify the muse—it's capricious. Just like people. Interrupting tasks and muscling aside thoughts, showing up when you can't easily deal with them.

I bless the muse when it comes as I stir soup just before the simmer. Or when I'm already at the computer, say, composing marginal emails. That's a thoughtful muse. Then I can catch the idea without a boatload of negative consequences.

**Prompt: Who or what is your muse?*

—May 31, 2015

The waddle of a happy woman*

On a spring night she entices tadpole-shaped life-givers into her body. Now she has everything she needs. It all develops nicely—amniotic fluid for floating, an umbilical cord for feeding, and elements like calcium for growing. A body expands inside her; not as a gift, but a force she beckoned into being.

She explodes into joy, grows big, huge, enormous, vast, full, expansive, all-encompassing, massive, colossal. She loves these descriptions, whispers them to herself in front of the mirror.

This is power and she knows it. No one else will or has or could produce the life she contains, the one protruding in front as she sways toward her future.

**From a prompt…*

There were things I told no one*

I told no one of how pragmatically I had considered doing away with myself—until a friend tried suicide and my story comforted her aloneness.

I told no one of my mid-life feelings of alienation from others, from myself. I didn't talk of profound aloneness or of my simultaneous need to reject and embrace that aloneness—until I told the friend of my heart, while I lay in the darkness, weeping, my head on his shoulder.

I told no one of the fear and sadness of motherhood, the ambivalence surrounding it—until my daughters and young friends gave birth. I couldn't leave them alone, as I had been, with those issues unspoken…

**Prompt: What things have you told no one?*

Why today?*

This morning's writing prompt was: "I had not expected…"

That seems clear enough. I take paper and pen, search out a comfortable chair in the sun, stare at the paper.

A path into this idea begins to materialize. Then my mind sits down, chin on hand, to think over various meanings and nuances of the word *expect*. It refuses to go farther. The path becomes a dead end.

Usually I can count on my brain, busy little thing.

But apparently a switch has been thrown and it's on a sidetrack this morning.

—March 2007

**Prompt from a poem: "I had not expected."*

An Artist's Prayer*

Creator God, artist of the worlds,
Let me feel your spirit moving across the waters of my spirit,
dividing me into day and night,
placing my stars in their courses,
creating living works to accompany me on my journey.

Let me feel your strong winds,
the rugged breath of your creativity
as I struggle to express my own.

Infuse me with your spirit,
keep me enthused.

And at the end, hold me in your heart gently —
for in the creative moment I am timeless,
still a vulnerable child
as I come again to you.

**Assignment from The Artist's Way, 1999*

Ten years before Betty Friedan kicked off women's liberation with Feminine Mystique, twenty years before Ms Magazine appeared, and more than a half century before Facebook COO Sheryl Sanders urged women to Lean In, lots of women in the so-called "silent generation" got the picture.

If we wanted, we pursued work before, during and after having our families. Many of us defined ourselves in terms of work and career, even if the world thought of us as "wife of" or "mother of."

These miniatures have a little different feel...a reflection of my more businesslike self.

—From a memoir-in-progress, 2011

Nothing like it

For those who prefer a public playing field to a private one (or are active in both), there is no substitute for professional competence.

It allows you to contribute what you have learned to help others, to accomplish goals, to perform work that is meaningful to you and people you work with. Once you've experienced those particular rewards, you tend to seek them again and again.

They are different from the private payback you get from rearing children successfully or sustaining a good relationship. I tend to think of those as learning-on-the-job activities...they're never over, always in progress. If you accomplish them well, eventually you may gain wisdom, but that is different from skill.

If you've gained skill at a task that's used to meet group goals—writing clear prose, coaching beginners with new jobs, programming electronic equipment, diagnosing and treating ailments, creating a piece of art—this gives you professional competence.

I believe there is no substitute for it, and those who have it will continue to seek ways to use it to their benefit and that of others.

—Feb. 2009

If you have a business... and yes, that means writers and artists, too.

- Starting a business, such as writing a book or composing a painting, is not a linear project. You can begin anywhere and proceed from there.
- Many people have good products or services. Fewer pay attention to their attitudes and mundane details, which is where success lies.
- You, and you alone, get to define "success" if you're working for yourself.
- You will need to enjoy designing your business and running it nearly as much as you enjoy creating your product or service.

Distilled from The Real American Dream, Creating Independence and Running a One-person Business

—1999

Naming your business

Throughout history and through many cultures naming has been synonymous with control and power.

The god who creates, names those creations. In Grimm's fairy tale, the miller's daughter gained power over Rumpelstiltskin simply by learning his name.

Think of naming your business in the same light. The power is yours. You create a business and you bestow a name. To a great extent, you will control how the public perceives you through the name you give your business. Don't do it lightly.

And please. Have your business name tell me what you do.

—2000

About meetings

"The person who goes into a meeting knowing what he or she wants, has the best chance of getting it."

A corporate executive responsible for international relations in a big firm told me that when I first moved into a management job. It helped me for years and came back to bite when I forgot it.

Of course, this is true of any gathering, corporate or not.

From parent-teacher meetings to boards of directors, it helps to know what you want from a meeting, even it it's nothing more than to move discussions along so you can get out on time.

—1980

How do you keep from flinching?

Little pieces of paper. They lie on my desk in small un-tidy piles, although some are tucked into envelopes labeled "keep." They hold brief bits of wisdom I wrote down when they came my way. They might be useful again.

The one below dates from my stint in the corporate world, because when I first read it, I believed it applies to life in general, not just the world of work. It's been in a little pile for many years, waiting. Recently I mailed it to a granddaughter in the Marines' Officer Candidate School…talk about needing not to flinch!

∞

Q: How do you keep from flinching?

A: The best insurance against flinching is not getting in over your head. This division has prided itself on having ambitious goals and conservative, short-term plans…If you set the plan too high and then don't reach it, you begin to flinch. By meeting short-term plans, confidence builds to the point that you can stay the course.

Tekweek, Feb. 21, 1992
From an interview with Roy Barker,
a GM in computer graphics group at Tektronix.

—2016

Walking in the rain

During my learning-to-be-corporate phase, I paid a lot of attention to how people presented themselves physically—men and women, young and old, on the street and at rest. I noticed posture, eye contact, what people did with their arms and hands, how they sat and walked and what I inferred from those things. I also tried to deduce what other people realized from those things.

I concluded that in the real world how you present yourself matters. It matters a lot if you want people to take you seriously.

The whole idea came together for me one day in downtown Portland. Jaywalkers ambled across the wide street as they headed to lunch from nearby offices. A light rain began. I took shelter beneath an awning and watched.

No one wore a raincoat or carried an umbrella—the shower fell unexpectedly. People had come from the same offices, walking alone or in groups of two or three. All wore suits or an equivalent, all stood the same chance of getting a little damp. Rain fell on the just and the unjust. But the men and women behaved differently.

The women—every one while I watched—ducked their heads, pulled in their shoulders and attempted to shrink. Many held a purse against their chests and folded their arms over it. Or held a purse over their heads with one hand while folding the other arm tightly over their chests. They began to scuttle—small hurrying steps.

The men walked as they had before the sprinkle began—heads up, shoulders back, arms swinging freely. The unsuited stuck their hands nonchalantly in pants pockets. They seemed undaunted by the few drops of rain.

I thought about this.

Before the rain, I had seen no material difference between these office workers, talking and laughing their way to lunch together. But when a few drops of water fell, the women diminished their appearance by attempting evasive action *that did no good*. They didn't get less wet than the men who strode beside them. They shrank from something unavoidable.

To my watching eyes, they became "less than," and I vowed to keep my head high, arms at my side or swinging loose, and to stride purposefully through every drop this rainy climate sent my way.

—From a memoir-in-progress, 2012

For creative types

Give your work away if you want, but don't sell it cheap.

—1989-2002

More than one string in your bow

When I was young, two of my dad's traits seemed contradictory.

He was a lover, not a fighter, this man who managed the AT&T telephone office in a small Nebraska town. His bailiwick included women operators and male linemen, equipment and customers, and occasionally contentious relationships with the smaller, locally-owned companies he called "farmer lines."

He disliked unhappy or difficult situations and I watched him avoid them when he could. But I noted he also had the ability to wade into action, settle disputes or respond graciously to troublesome conditions when he felt it necessary.

When avoidance would have made a labor dispute last longer, or when dodging a heated discussion would have damaged the company or his personal ethics, he buckled down and dealt with people firmly and fairly.

Thus I learned that effective people have more than one way of responding to events.

—From a memoir in progress, 2016

Sunday Morning Problem-Solving

My office has been resisting me lately.

I enter to write or think and end up checking e-mail or playing some of the thirty-six varieties of solitaire on my computer. Soon this gives me a headache, so I leave with no project moving ahead, no gain against the entropy of life.

"My office" sounds singular, but it's not. Linked to the main house by a small room full of plants, it spans two rooms. The first room doesn't push me away. I can write there or read the current *New Yorker.* It's where I raise the flip chart, grip colored markers and consult with friends or family. I pay bills and write notes at the oak and pecan desk. This room nurtures me, I do good work there; it feels alive.

Ahhh. That's the word I need this morning, *alive.* The sitting room-office breathes with colors, textures, warm woods, good art; the office-office is sterile. It's wonderfully organized and efficient, but the energy has dwindled since I'm no longer running a business from it.

Well, I can fix that.

I turn the small Bose to the classical music station and fill my air space with Beethoven's sublime violin concerto in D Major. I wind the antique clock and set its pendulum in motion, adding both sound and movement with one stroke. I light a candle scented with night-blooming jasmine. Then I find a glossy-leaved rubber plant and place it by a window. That does it.

The room has life now; creativity will follow.

—2007

Travel takes many shapes: downtown to shop, month-long trips to exotic lands for vacation, business trips. The Nebraskans I know travel widely, curious to check out the world, happy to come home. I still feel like one of them, although I've lived in the Northwest most of my adult life.

Here are vignettes from different kinds of travel, starting with a series about flying to the Far East for business on the classic old Pan Am trans-Pacific flights in the mid-eighties. Flying was fun in the days before 9/11, TSA, and paranoia.

Business class

Pan American Airways flew the Pacific routes in those days. The name Pan Am invoked the idea of glamorous travel to exotic destinations. I loved the giant silver planes with their two-story interiors and crisply efficient navy-blue suited attendants still called stewardesses. Or people were beginning to use the strange word, stewardae, to show that we were hip frequent fliers.

The business section often occupied the second floor of Boeing's bulbous 747s, offering me a roomy respite between months of planning and the coming excitement of executing the game plan in Taipei, Seoul, Hong Kong.

These trans-Pacific flights even now are among the longest any airline flies to anywhere—fifteen, sixteen, eighteen hours—time enough for stories to begin and end, time enough to fully inhabit a world of strangers.

Maybe other women passengers lounged in first class—slim young things traveling on the arm of alpha males. Or maybe they squirmed in coach—traveling home from visiting children or grandchildren in the States. But in the mid-1980s, I was one of very few women in business class.

This was not new for me; my working life always had been spent with men. And now, in my fifties, in the flying cocoon of Pan Am, I could enjoy the process of establishing myself with strangers. Or not. My choice.

—1980s Above the Pacific

Business class: I knew he would

On my first trip—Portland-Seattle-Japan-Taipei—a good-looking seven-footer from the East Coast stood out.

He flew the route so often he knew the cabin crew by name. He displayed a comfortably proprietary manner, as if he owned the plane and was hosting us. He walked up and down the aisles, stretching his long legs, talking with other regulars. Their ease indicated they could have dropped into the corner coffee shop instead of racing a third of the way around the world at thirty-six thousand feet.

Early on he marched around with someone's disgruntled baby on his shoulder. He patted and cooed until she slept, then handed her back to her tired mother, the only other woman around. Then he slept, stretched over most of a row of center seats with arm-rests folded back.

He and I talked, exchanging business cards by way of introduction. I mentioned wanting to pick up a pair of cheap knock-off walking shoes. He said Korea was the place for those, what size did I wear? He'd get me a pair, and deliver them to my Taipei hotel. No, he wouldn't take money now, he'd collect if he could get the shoes. He left the plane in Tokyo to connect to Seoul.

Days later he showed up at my hotel, delivered the shoes, collected his eleven dollars and wished me well, thereby astonishing my manager who had told me, "You're so naïve. He'll never show up."

—1985 Over the Pacific

Business class: American women

"Y'know," he said, "a lot of the guys fly Singapore because of the girls." He was referring to the world-class beauties in traditional dress who light up Singapore Airlines with their petite elegance.

"But not me. I want these strong-minded Pan Am women around if something goes wrong."

He was another of the chatty fraternity of regular business travelers on the Far-East routes and he told this story of an incident he'd observed:

The flight had been delayed because several male passengers, all Indians, had refused to buckle their seat belts. They became belligerent, perhaps because the order was given by a woman. A senior stewardess won the face-off when she refused to okay takeoff unless they complied. Faced with her ultimatum and muttering from other passengers, the men buckled up.

But it was a strategic retreat, lasting only until they were in the air.

Then they moved out of their seats, sat down cross-legged in the aisle, and prepared to light the charcoal braziers they had brought to cook their own food.

The storyteller's question was rhetorical: "Now what do you think those dainty little Asian girls would have done with blocked aisles, a fire hazard and several large unruly men?"

He swept on. "Those American women just waded in. They confiscated the cooking stuff. When the Indians refused to clear the aisle, I'll be damned if this one gal didn't pick up a guy—a big guy—and manhandle him back into his seat. It sure made the rest of them move."

He grinned at the memory. "You bet. Give me American women every time."

Nearly fifteen years later I remembered this conversation when I read about the flight attendants who called in valuable information as their planes headed for the twin towers.

And those who helped take down the Pennsylvania flight.

—1987 Over the Pacific

Business class: Avon, really?

On my second trip to Taiwan, I sat beside a woman in the business section. She looked some twenty-plus years younger than I. She'd left children at home in the care of a husband. An auditor for Avon, she was on a regular trip to review the company books in Taipei before flying on to Hong Kong for more of the same.

I expressed surprise, because I thought the company was fading badly in the US. But she said Avon was very big in the Far East. Seems their soap is great for silk.

—1985, Over the Pacific

Business class: ... how you play the game.

During a flight to Hong Kong from Seoul, I sat by a tall man from India. Preliminary conversation revealed he had just medaled in shooting in the Tenth Asian Games held in South Korea in 1986.

Sports is an easy topic for creating rapport with men and I often used it in the game of "establish your credentials," a business version of cocktail chatter. So I mentioned that a young woman from my home state of Nebraska had won gold in rifle marksmanship at the previous Olympics and asked if he'd met her. He had.

I mentioned I could shoot a rifle and that I'd also used a shotgun hunting pheasants in the autumn stubble fields of Midwest farmland.

He seemed surprised that I knew about the medalist and that I used to handle the long guns. He himself was a handgun person.

Prepared to be further impressed, my seatmate asked what my position was in my company. I answered that I had been a mid-level manager and was now scouting out Korea and Hong Kong in advance of future trips.

"Right now I'm an individual without a department or a budget," I told him truthfully. "Very low on the ladder in a very big corporation."

"Nonsense," he said, rather brusquely. "You're joking with me."

He gave me a sharp look before he turned away. "You are at least a vice-president."

And with that settled we went back to our reading.

Well, I thought rather smugly, *I've got that part of this job aced. Dress the part, talk their language, be confident. Suddenly you're a VP!*

—1986 Over the Pacific

Departure (Seoul)

A bomb had exploded the week before. Now the airport was patrolled by Korean soldiers in twos, marching in step. The air turned chill as they passed.

They stood well over six feet tall and solid. They wore black uniforms, trousers bloused into black combat boots. Their faces were grim and their machine guns cradled at the ready.

Work finished, nostalgic for home, the engineers, managers and I sat down to a fast-food meal, our first in nearly two weeks.

We talked about events we hadn't anticipated. One member of our team had been stopped by armed guards on a public street near the President's house because he carried a video camera. We discussed dictatorship, street markets with kittens in cages, the lack of dogs.

Several burgers stayed suspended in mid-air when one of the guys looked at the half-eaten bun in his hand and said thoughtfully, "I don't know what it is, but it isn't beef."

—April 1987 Seoul, Korea

I love USPS

I just purchased two stamps at the hotel's front desk. They cost me less than a dollar and ensure the safe delivery of two birthday notes from my hands in Lihue, Kauai, to two separate mailboxes in the environs of Portland, Oregon. That's 2,624 miles across the Pacific in a day or two.

I can't think why some people complain about the US postal service. How can you beat that?

—Kauai, November, 2013

Terror in the sky

The pilot, I'll call him Harry, walked across the sun-bathed Hawaiian tarmac toward us after saying goodbye to his passengers. Tall, broad-shouldered, rumpled dark blonde hair, leather bomber jacket, boots, and was that a swagger? Yes it was, a suggestion of Harrison Ford. He lacked only a white silk scarf.

Marge from Minnesota, the other woman set to fly with us, and I saw him at the same time. As our eyes met, I nodded in appreciation, "Oh, this is going to be just fine!"

How wrong could I be?

We were about to join Harry in his helicopter for a door-less ride over Kauai. Yes, that's right, an hour in a Hughes 500 with NO DOORS. It had a big rotor overhead and a small one on the tail. Two passengers and Harry would sit thigh to thigh in the front seat, two in the back.

Marge sat front middle, next to Harry's thigh. This gave me the right side. The one with the handhold over the missing door. A helper wedged me into double shoulder straps anchored to a wide belt secured with a fist-sized knob. The knob fit just under the life vest packet also strapped around my waist "in the unlikely event of a water landing."

I noted that my harness and Harry's were identical. My mind understood that if the webbing was good enough for the pilot, it would keep me in place.

However, my body didn't get it. It thought I was holding myself in with my hand above the open doorway.

My mind also understood the upbeat commentary reaching me from Harry through the Bose noise-dampeners on my ears. And my eyes registered the deep blue Pacific lapping hidden coves on the NaPali coast, and eight-stage waterfalls lacing through the green of Waialiali crater.

But my body? Frozen in place from the early moment when Harry said cheerfully, "I'll do a little S curve here so you can see the spouting horn better." Then he let us see Waimea canyon, the cliffs and the crater waterfalls better. Each new scenic wonder caused him to tip me toward my missing door. My body knew that only my hand grip and braced body kept me from falling into the luscious green below.

After a full hour of this, my brain registered our perfect landing. But again, my body refused to believe it and would not move. Someone else had to unbuckle me, saying, "Here, take my hand," and guiding my feet to the step stool, hence to the tarmac where we'd started.

—November, 2013

I may never get to Petra

Leaving Gunnison, Colorado, the road rapidly rose to nine thousand feet. We drove past working cowboys and their cattle at that surprising level, then dropped through the green sage and red, yellow, blue and purple wildflowers of a wet spring, took the Moab turnoff.

I may never get to Petra, a city carved by people into high walls of pink limestone in Jordan. But I will be content with the blazing red spires and pinnacles, castles and fortresses carved by wind, cold and heat in the canyons that met us that day.

This deep valley country felt larger, more spectacular, wilder and more dangerous than Sedona. It seemed very near creation, breathing hot spirit-earth power.

In the spike and turret-encrusted heart of the canyon we got out of the car to look up. The fierce red heat enfolded us, cradled our little human bodies.

Back in the car we left the windows wide open, loath to give up the nurturing feeling. Yes, we left the air conditioning on—it was at least a hundred degrees outside. But our hair blew in the wind. Not completely encased in our metal and glass tube we felt more connected to the primal countryside.

The road dropped fast and met the river. Flowing wide and calm through the canyons, the brick-red Colorado in mid-summer showed no sign of the power that had carved the Grand Canyon downstream. Today it serenely entertained groups of rafters as colorful as the rocks around them. Some had left their bright blue boats to float alone, buoyed by fat red life vests.

We continued our descent to the junction where we would turn right. The landscape cooled to buff and blue. Soon one right after the other came two gigantic gully-washing rains powered by sky-to-earth jags of hot lightening and wake-the-dead thunderclaps. The finale to this day in the canyon felt near creation again.

—July 17, 2013

Snapshot June 2008

Jim and I snuggled up to the trunk of a thick-leaved tree as warm rain poured around us in San Rafael, a resort town on the Mediterranean near Cannes. We'd arrived the day before from Nice, planning to travel alone to five countries in five weeks.

The mistral arrived about when we did. The locals told us it would blow for three days. We didn't care, we stood together at the beginning of an adventure.

—San Rafael, France, late May 2008

In a fine rain one day, Isabella told us

In Tuscany if the cave in the rock hillside has a curved top, if it's maybe twice as wide as tall, with a bit of a suggestion that humans shaped it, if on close inspection you see the cave has a three- or four- or maybe six-inch channel dug into the center of the floor, if this indentation leads to the front edge of the opening and you can imagine water dribbling or cascading from it into a miniature water fall, it's an Etruscan tomb.

—Near Piensa, Italy, June 2008

Winged Victory

I've never been a road to Damascus person. I learn by increments, not great revelations.

Still, I learned everything about female power and its beauty in one heart-stopping moment when, at the age of forty, I rounded a corner in the Louvre. There, at the top of the majestic Daru staircase, framed by classic arches and gleaming in natural lighting, stood the Winged Victory of Samothrace.

Wings aloft, she faced into the wind. It swirled her garments and plastered them tight to her body, clarifying its strength.

—Autumn 1972

Beginning reporters always get to write obituaries. On the paper where I started, the other newbie job was being the "Ain't Nature Grand!" editor. I minded it less than the obits, because yes, nature is grand…a huge part of my life, then and now. These vignettes reflect some of my lifelong amazement.

If I lived alone, in four parts

Summer

I'd never go anywhere.

I'd wear old clothes to my office. There I'd open wide every window and both doors to sweet heat smells and little breezes, so trifling they don't even ruffle paper.

Until late afternoon I'd write down every thought that entered my mind, moving between blue gel pens on lined paper and the elegant Mac.

Afterward a friend would come to the lower yard. We'd sit in the Adirondack chairs beneath the pine with russet branches and silver-tinged needles. We'd sip Red Zinger tea, iced, with lemon, and read each other the words we found earlier that day. The exchange would be easy and light. It would be many ways warm.

Then the friend would leave.

Later that night, I'd pad barefoot to the deck, stretch out on the chaise and say goodnight to the Milky Way.

Fall

"In autumn, one is not confused by activity and green leaves." Another Nebraskan, Loren Eiseley, said that.

Like Eiseley, I find it easy to focus in the fall. Like the tangy apples ripening in my lower yard, I'd gain crispness while the air cooled, colors changed and energy flowed, replacing summer's lethargy. I'd become a frugal gardener, laying by carrots, potatoes, and onions to carry me through the winter,

I'd design dinner parties for six or eight, keyed to the last flowers of fall in their Florentine colors, gold and purple, deep red and orange. Gold candles would glow on the table that holds crown roast of pork with gingered fruit. Courvoisier later in the living room.

When alone again, I'd read by the fire.

Sometimes all night.

Winter

If I lived alone at Christmas I wouldn't travel with strangers to warmth and forced gaiety. I'd stay in the Northwest's cold, grey rain.

Most mornings I'd dress in two layers and waterproof shoes and walk into the chill. I'd return refreshed. With wind-whipped energy I'd call a few friends, plan my evening.

As the day darkened, surrounded by boisterous Renaissance holiday music and candle-whiffs of bayberry, I'd light a fire. Fruity aromas spiked with juniper would drift from the Della Robbia mantel. I'd prepare eggnog, thick with French vanilla ice cream and lots of brandy for two or three friends. I'd add enough of Vicktor's holiday pate, seven-year-old cheddar and crackers to keep winter at bay. We'd hear the echo of ancient solstice celebrations.

Alone again, as candles guttered, I'd let silence resume and the tears would come. I would weep for the other Christmas, with its foreshadowing birth.

I'd cry for the babies.

Spring

In spring the exploding green world would keep me company. Fat grey-tailed squirrels, trembly-legged twin fawns, and the first robins would appear along with a shuffling raccoon I would have to trap if he stayed around.

During warming solitary days I'd watch as branch-end chartreuse clumps on the giant fir tree turned into fuzzy tips that spread yellow dust over the deck and chairs and made me sneeze.

Following white, lemon and lavender crocuses, midnight-blue hyacinths would bloom. They'd provide a sweet and tangy perfume for my bedroom to vie with an occasional acrid whiff from the skunk who ambles past after dark, peering from my deck through the French door. What is she looking for?

And when I curled up alone at the end of the day, I'd murmur into the pillow, *you are so brave.*

—Summer, 2001

Deadheading

I listen to the wind gusting high overhead in the pines and think wistfully of fishing in mountain streams with that familiar sound above.

Instead, I am cleaning up rhododendrons festooned with six-inch needle-pairs that have landed upside down on every branch, having drifted down from the pines I just admired. The needles make my lovely bushes look scruffy.

Shall I detach every one of those hundreds of brown pine hairpins, or wait for the autumn winds to remove them?

I sigh, leave the needles, and begin to deadhead the eight-foot rhodies. This is a task I like—tidying the bush by snapping off dead blossoms. It creates a lot of visual payoff for very little labor.

I murmur quietly to the giant I'm working on, "Oh, you are going to look so much better. You'll love it."

Then I glance around to see if anyone hears me talking to the plants.

—Spring 1998

Flamingos in the desert

Flamingos at a distance form lovely pink islands, or wide, flat pink clouds in the sky. Up close and individually they become funny-looking birds.

A few dozen strut around in tight groups in a resort pond four or five feet from where I've flopped onto a bench to cool down after a brisk walk.

The longer I look, the funnier they seem. I start to smile to myself.

They have pink knees like round doorknobs.

They hold their heads tipped back at the angle of someone reading through the bottom section of bifocal lenses.

Their black beaks start out going straight ahead, as beaks should, then angle sharply down, as if the designer changed his mind.

One feeding pink bird has his head completely under water, prancing around it in a circle of little steps. Around and around he goes, as if he's a living screwdriver, twisting his beak firmly into the Marriott lake bottom.

—Palm Desert, February 2013

I could not live

I have never lived in a house without plants and I could not. Years ago I hauled a scraggly philodendron named "Tuni," (short for Petunia), all over the country to insure I'd have a plant when I got to where I was going.

A home without plants is missing a vital ingredient for me. Yes, they require care (except Tuni, who needed very little and who liked travel). But also they thoughtfully re-oxygenate the air. They soften rigid tables or desks, supply angles and edges where some strength of character is missing in the furnishings. But mostly they add life.

I love to buy or receive a small plant and grow it into a healthy adult. I also like to rescue poorly cared for plants, neglected ones.

I thought my relationship with houseplants was private until one day a friend showed up at my house carrying a straggly, brown-around-the-edges Boston fern, a mop of neediness.

"Happy birthday," she trilled. "I saw this in the shop and knew you could nurse it back to health."

—November, 1972

Maybe we should...

"Maybe we should keep life lists and join the Audubon Society, know what birds we're looking at in an informed way," I muse aloud.

We are sitting at the morning table, drinking green tea and watching orioles (yellow), house finches (red), the occasional flicker (black-bib), while noting the splendid arrival and abrupt departure of Anna's hummingbirds.

I persist. "Is it a failing that we don't get left-brained about all this?" My gesture includes plants, birds, squirrels, small animals under and over ground.

I don't get much response, so continue the conversation with myself:

We don't save our years worth of symphony or theater programs and catalogue them, either. Often in the first bar or two I recognize Mozart, Dvorak, Beethoven and Tchaikovsky, among others. I know Harold Pinter's works before I arrive at the theater. Often I know Sibelius, pick up a reference to Arthur Miller.

But to name and date each work, each bird, to have them in order in my mind, or on a shelf for reference—I don't do it.

Instead, I opt for enjoying movement, color, size differences, attitudes (those jays are cocky). Evocations without labels.

Living in the moment? Or lazy?

—Summer 2009

Spring

Spring can be a weird, rambunctious time, full of breathtaking beauty and excitement. When rising sap in trees coincides with rising hormones in budding bodies, spring can make you ache with longing.

I remember.

But another face of spring is a gift to the not-so-young. It follows the first series of flowers, when the blossoming work of tulips and flowering plum is finished. The broad-leafs have become broad indeed, and winter-weary conifers have freshened themselves with tassels of chartreuse at the end of each branch.

A day of stillness arrives. A day of warm air stirring so slightly the movement needs another name—breeze is too strong for these gentle puffs. Suburban mowers and blowers are absent, their work done yesterday.

On such a day to sit on the deck in the silence feels like a sacrament.

—May 2007

Springtime growth

I dropped my arms and stood panting, staring as tiny drops of blood rose to my skin in protest where blackberry thorns had ripped my old shirt. My scalp felt the first damp prickles of sweat. Soon they would pool and run slowly under my hair. The sun, behind thin clouds, gloomed the ground but did nothing to cool it.

In the thicket, malignant cane ropes, dense with new life, climbed overhead and up into the apple tree, blurring its outlines, competing for sunlight.

I couldn't dismantle the tangle methodically. Vines went everywhere, over, around and under. They formed arches of acid green intertwined with smaller and larger arcs. They rooted right and left, in front and behind me. Every place I'd cut them last week, every joint in the vine, sprouted vigorous, foot-long, multi-branched growth.

I cut at eye level. I stretched overhead to pull vines down, bent to pull roots not yet solidly in place, applied random cuts, fancied the mass was growing in the hot, humid air even as I tried to cut it back. I wanted this nasty thing gone.

As the day heated up my body wilted along with my psyche. Working with clippers, my arms tired, hands lost grip through their sturdy leather coverings. Once again I understood I would not tame this virulent mess with the tools and energy at hand. I could cut and slash, even poison it, but it would win. Its life-force would outlast mine. I knew this from other years, other attempts to tame this same vine. I continued to cut and chop, losing conviction.

Later my cell phone rang as I drank iced tea on the deck. A friend's diagnosis had been confirmed: her melanoma, beaten back twice, had returned in force. Growing so fast, rooted in so many places, tangled in lungs and breathing spaces too deeply, it could not be removed.

Months, they told her. Just months.

—May 2008

Two takes on one photo

"Now that's my idea of hell," she says, punctuating with a mock shudder.

A Seattle friend, native of the Northwest, is responding to a photo on my computer showing a glittering ice field reflecting a weak sun. The ice field covers a central Nebraska farm.

Nebraskans are busy emailing photos like this to each other daily—devastating ice storms have frozen the prairie country, knocking out power, isolating farms and cities, stopping everything.

In the center of the gleaming stubblefield on my screen lies a downed transmission tower, felled by ice thick enough to topple a Douglas fir. The fields are table-top flat, they flow across the photo, presenting no edges left, right or bottom, to stop your eye. Only if you stare long enough, do you notice the Monopoly-sized buildings of a farm on the horizon.

I feel the emptiness, hear the silence and my protest comes involuntarily: "It's magnificent!"

—January 2007

Who does understand?

I spend a lot of time looking out my windows into what I playfully call our wildlife refuge. In reality, it's a big suburban yard on the edge of a bit of open ground.

I understand much of what I see: the deer who eats the last of the apples in fall reappears in summer with twin fawns; ground-feeding birds clean the grass under the feeder suspended above them.

But I don't understand the ebb and flow of populations over the years. One year we heard nothing of the woeful mourning dove mating call that means spring. A neighbor said red-tailed hawks were abundant that year. Now the doves are back, and yet I see an abundance of red-tails swooping over the trees in the sky outside every window.

I'm looking at a squirrel, a slim streak of dark brown, almost the color of the bark, motionless against a tree trunk. He's one of the interlopers who arrived maybe four years ago and multiplied, driving the larger grey fellows from our yard.

I read that the small dark squirrels are fierce, and tend to replace the more benign locals. They appeared to do just that, year after year chasing each other up and down the tall firs, chewing their way under the house, scattering pink insulation around the yard while the beauties with fat tails the size of their bodies almost disappeared.

But something has happened, and the little dark squirrel I'm watching seems alone, while the great grey tails frolic everywhere.

—November 2006

Like tapas in Spain, here are some unrelated observations. Again like tapas, you can dip into just one for an appetizer, or put several together for a more substantial repast. Most of these, in one way or another, relate to families.

Contentment

Contentment with the status quo never was celebrated as a goal in the stories told and re-told in my family.

—2016

Top quarter of the tank

I prefer to drive my car on the top quarter of the tank of gas. Not for me the slide on fumes into the last gas station on the edge of town. I've done it, but no more.

By the same token, I prefer each day to reserve enough energy to deal with the unexpected occurrence that will require my presence or input. One often comes.

—2016

A truth

Women must write their own stories if they want to be known. No one else will do it for them.

From a memoir-in-progress, 2013

I prefer words

Numbers slide through my mind like schools of silvery fish. They look alike, flow together and separate, merge, pull apart, re-merge.

I've confronted each in its time: mortgages, salaries, vacation dates, birthdays (parents, children, friends, husbands, co-workers), 401K contributions, social security, telephones (land line, cell, spouse, neighbors, kids, friends, frequently called), stock prices, the number portion of my license plate. Grocery, restaurant, hardware, makeup, clothing and shoe prices. Tickets for airplanes, sports events, concerts and the Nutcracker.

Slipping through, they make no impression, leave no memory for later recall.

—May, 2010

Like

In a small town, "like" is not much of a factor. You get along with everyone because there aren't lots of people to choose among.

It's good training for corporate life. Or life in general, for that matter.

—2000s

Of course

People who say, *…and I'm not going to talk about it!* always do.

—1999

Beds

Some people leap out of them happily but I don't want to leave my bed in the morning. Any bed, anywhere. Any morning. A bed is a beautiful thing and I want to stay attached as long as possible.

Yet once I crept out before dawn to drive over the Berkeley hills to an Easter sunrise service followed by gin fizzes at brunch.

Once I moaned from a sleeping bag at two a.m. to force down pancakes and eggs before climbing eight hours up a glaciated mountain.

Many times I staggered alone out of a warm double bed to nurse a daughter at four a.m.

I remember a Swiss feather bed with ironed linens, a wood fake antique on the third floor of a Paris hotel where the electricity failed, and one of those sleep-number mattresses that fairly shrieked as air pumped into it in an Oregon coast rental.

In childhood a carved walnut bed held me tight in mornings after I'd read too late the night before. In the 1970s a ten-dollar, sloshing waterbed cradled me fondly.

Beds always have offered me peace and sanctuary and warmth—bless them.

—2001

Morning has broken

As awareness begins its low seep, I scrunch my eyelids together like a child. I want to hold onto sleep, to grab it with both hands and pull it back over me like a blanket that begins to slide away.

Morning is here again, and I want to postpone its arrival. I've never been able to, but I keep trying.

My dream world fast-fades. Quickly…can I put myself back into it and continue the story?

No. No matter how I concentrate, Dream slides away to join Sleep in a magic land I can't access again until tonight.

—2009

Stored away

I have stored away in the nooks and crannies of my brain—or should I say in the dendrites and neural storage spots—perfect images of my friends, children, parents, places.

I don't have access to them during the day, but they're available to my dreaming self.

—December, 2013

Naps

Nap *days* come in delicious varieties. Our two Pacific Northwest weather categories are "grey" and "bright" and each works just fine for sleeping.

On a grey day, it seems right to find a soft pillow and an alpaca throw to snuggle into. I pull it over my ears like a mummy-style sleeping bag.

On a bright day, it seems decadent to darken the room and lie down, because in this climate everyone knows you should be working, playing or doing something active when the sun is out.

Similarly, nap *places* vary. I stretch out on a blue down-filled sofa in the living room, or curl onto the loveseat in my office. Sometimes I flop diagonally across the king-sized bed, taking up as much space as possible.

There also are nap *accoutrements,* such as pillows and covers that define both temperature and mood. Surrounded by books in my office, I can lie under a fringed throw woven to depict more books and use the Siamese cat pillow. Since my temperature drops to hibernation when I sleep, even a hot day requires a cover. It would preferably be sheer and pretty.

Nap *situations* vary, too. They can be a response to fatigue, or an indulgence.

The main thing about a nap is that it doesn't resemble going to bed at night.

For example, I toured a home with a woman of wealth and in her airy, elegant bedroom the covers were folded back in a triangle to reveal ironed white sheets. A smooth rose night gown was laid out for her. She explained the housekeeper already had turned the bed down in preparation for her afternoon nap.

Now that, for me, is not napping. It's going to bed

in the middle of the day, which should be saved for the occasional headache or flu.

The science, or maybe it's art, of nap-taking has not been documented that I know of. Any such book would involve subjects such as creativity (sign on closed door: *Writer at work*), or retreat from responsibility *(Hush, Mommy's sleeping).*

I must write that book some afternoon when I'm not napping.

—Several years in the 2000s

Condiments

If life is a steak, people are the béarnaise sauce on top to enrich it further. If life is a bowl of creamy broccoli-spinach soup, people are the cumin and nutmeg that spice it. If life is a papaya, people are the generous squeeze of lime that enlivens it.

But reality isn't all béarnaise, spices and lime. Too much, and the original flavor is masked or overpowered.

So it is with me and people. I like most people; I love many. I value contact with differing personalities, ideas and experiences. I'm not anti-social. But too many people mask the life I should be living, a life without pressure, an ordinary life with an everyday smoothness of tasks.

Too many people change the flavor that is right for me.

But if I've gone too long without them, I get dull, like a steak without sauce, soup without spices and fruit without lime.

—2014

Dealing with complexity

Going through old college materials I came across a paper boldly titled: *What is the Matter with France?*

I answered the question in sixteen double-spaced typewritten pages, plus one for a bibliography. What courage. What chutzpah. What a laugh.

I opened another box to find a different paper, from another year, another class titled *What I Am Like and Why I Am That Way.*

That took only eight double-spaced, typewritten pages and required no bibliography.

Clearly I am not as complex as France.

—1953-2009

Do you talk to your computer?

It's taken a while to develop, but I have come to an understanding of the bond I want with my equipment. It differs from my connection with human beings.

With machinery or technology—any thing designed to perform a function—I don't want an equal relationship. I don't want give and take from both sides. I want to be in charge. Always. I figure equipment exists only to make my life easier.

I want machinery (clothes drier, stove and leaf blower, computer, printer, wifi and cell phone) to work the same way every time. I want it to use the capacity built into it by the mind of an engineer and the factory to do its job flawlessly time after time.

I don't expect that of people; I'm well aware we are products of a much messier and less predictable process, therefore prone to make mistakes, to be inconsistent or to malfunction at awkward times.

I don't anthropomorphize mechanical or technological things. I'm sure about the difference between humans and equipment. I cut people slack; they're like me, and heaven knows I need people to give me the benefit of the doubt.

But machinery, well, I don't want to be surprised by it, to find it broken or malfunctioning when I need it, or to have to approach it differently today than I did yesterday. I want consistency of performance; I want to be able to count on it.

When this doesn't happen I behave erratically, like a human being whose expectations and desires have been thwarted. Sometimes I get rid of machines after one chance at repair. Before their time, you could say. I've cried in frustration, I've sworn at high volume, I've switched brands. I've done without.

Some things I don't do. I don't talk to my computer or smart phone. I give them no slack, even though I know they were programmed and built by human beings. So was my washing machine, and it manages to perform week after week.

That's all I want. Consistency.

—1990-2016

Forty, fifty, sixty

Turning forty, I looked over my life, as many people do on momentous dates. I asked myself, "You may be half way through your life. Do you want the second half to look like the first half?"

The answer arrived by itself: "No."

In quick succession I took a full time job, initiated a divorce, re-married and moved to another state, thus ensuring that the second half of my life would be more frightening, more fun and less predictable than the first. I've never looked back.

At fifty, memories started to show up like unexpected visitors at my door:

A ten-year-old me stood in the gutter in front of my house, arms stretched to the sky above in joy, feet covered to the ankles by warm rushing water, soaked by a thunderstorm on a hot August Nebraska night.

I watched in amazement at our lace-covered dining room table as Uncle Ralph topped his dessert—hot apple pie—with leftover gravy from the Thanksgiving turkey. Like all my Bohemian uncles he was a force of nature.

As my ankles wobbled, I shivered and set off across the ice in new white shoe skates while better athletes glided ahead on the frozen wetland field we called Lake Seldom. Later we huddled before the bonfire on the bank with cocoa and marshmallows.

With the memories came an understanding: I must write these, preserve them in case someone wants to know about a Midwestern childhood. I will call the book, "Growing Up Rich." I'm working on it now.

At sixty, I breathed a new freedom. Running my own business, excited about the future, I felt like a space ship atop a rocket on a launch pad. I knew when the massive supports fell away shortly I'd lift off into another adventure. I had no idea what it would be, but I felt joyous and ready.

—November, 1992

About motherhood, circa 1959

I could discuss Sun Yat-sen, the rape of Nanking, the French and Russian revolutions, several wars and the Treaty of Versailles, but children were pretty much unknowns.

From memoir-in-progress, 2011

Earth mothers, a personal take

Women who aspire to be earth mothers should be more relaxed than I am.

From memoir-in-progress, 2011

Gratitude

An attitude of gratitude. We make a choice on that one, I think.

Most emotions arise spontaneously, like wisps of clouds in a blue sky. We notice them, but we don't cause them. Hunger, sadness, a giggle—we recognize them, we don't will them.

But gratitude seems more complex, some combination of thought and feeling, at some level, deciding to be grateful for our lives instead of regretful or whiney or sad.

Eventually, if we will ourselves into gratitude, it can become spontaneous. But it seems to me it takes a decision followed by practice and more practice, to feel grateful in the moment.

Another thing: Gratitude must go deeper than simply acknowledging good fortune, or it's too cheap. We eventually can learn to appreciate not only a drift of night-blooming jasmine but the uses of adversity and heart-stopping fear.

—*May 2007*

How does it work?

I'm in my office making calls. On the phone with a client, I hear her voice, and nothing else except the forever background hum of electronic gadgets and appliances.

Then I know—not guess, not think, but *know*—I am no longer alone in the house.

This isn't a scary story—it was simply my husband, returning from a breakfast meeting.

But how did I know with such confidence? He entered a door in another part of the house, too far away for me to hear.

I'm guessing this acute certainty, this awareness, must be left over from the pre-language stage of human development. The woman who could sense the presence of a soft-footed cougar entering her cave might protect herself and survive. The hunter feeling another man by him could determine friend or foe and possibly live longer.

—February 2007

Independent streak

As an infant I lay on a cotton quilt by the south window in our small, tidy house, the winter sun warming my bare skin. Mom said the sunlight was a good source of Vitamin D and that moving freely was fine exercise. While she sat on the carved beige carpet beside me, I waved my arms and legs and learned to roll over without impediment, warm and cared for, safe and nourished into freedom.

What a contrast to the idea of swaddling.

Like my mother, I preferred joyfully easing my babies into the world instead of helping them pretend they were not yet born. I similarly unbound my three daughters, let them move and kick and go without clothing. I didn't learn embarrassment at home; neither did they.

I became a child with an independent streak that in my mind dates all the way back to these pre-speech, pre-crawling days.

From a memoir-in-progress, 2014

I wanted to be Dorothy Parker

Dorothy Parker's first little book of poems, *Enough Rope,* is one of two volumes that got me though college. The other was by Ogden Nash, but he's another subject. Parker's cynical point of view and cleverness, her pals at the Algonquin, her big-city sparkle and life lived on an edge inspired envy in my twenty-year-old heart.

I fervently wanted to be Dorothy Parker. I wanted to be a writer no one could discuss without using the word "witty." I wanted famous friends and fame. But I knew Dorothy Parker died, and not well.

When Nora Ephrom told Charlie Rose, "I wanted to be Dorothy Parker," I figured I knew a lot about the young Nora. So of course I wanted to be Nora Ephrom. But then Nora died too.

I haven't found anyone with the appeal of those two, so I guess I'll have to concentrate on being me.

—2012

I want a Schwinn

Some people want equipment to run flawlessly, to be solid and efficient and always "on." They ride Schwinn bicycles. They're not beautiful, but you don't need to worry about them getting goosey and quitting on you. These people also buy sedans from reputable makers.

Other people are tinkerers. They ride Raleighs, or 18-speed racing bikes. If something goes wrong—and it will—they whip out the expensive tool kit they always carry and fix it. They know how. They love the process. They also buy Ferraris and such.

Those people also use Google Plus, the holy grail of web tinkerers. Always in beta, always changing—unannounced—always screwing up the formatting even if you followed directions flawlessly. I'm headed back to Facebook.

—2013

I'll take predictable any day

The Oregonian book reviewer searched his mind for an analogy to use in a book review and came up with this: "It flattened out, like Nebraska, and became predictable."

The comment started me off on an imaginary rant in defense of my state. I sat that reviewer down in front of my imagination and began on him:

"What, I ask you, is wrong with predictable? Predictable is lack of chaos, of turmoil, of disturbance.

"An oil spill in the Gulf of Mexico is unpredictable...do you prefer that? What about earthquakes, forest fires, the status of the opium crop in Afghanistan, an unruly stock market? What about ring-of-fire Pacific mountains like St. Helens, taking lives and livelihoods? Or go back farther to the eruption that buried Pompeii and the Santorini one that caused the seas to roll over half of Crete? Want that?

"Speaking of natural disasters, do you look forward to that big undersea earthquake they tell us is 'unpredictable' but inevitable in the Cascadia subduction zone off the Oregon coast? The one that will create tsunamis to devastate and change the coastline of two states?

"In fact, Mr. Book Reviewer, what about maybe ten thousand dead and lost in just such a quake in Japan? Plus that bit about a second Chernobyl? Prefer that?"

I had another point to make: "You think the Midwest is predictable because you see just the surface—long miles of flat prairie, now converted to corn fields. But you should know those plains hold potential for arbitrary catastrophes as wide as the horizon: plagues of grasshoppers, tornados, blizzards that whiten and shut down areas bigger than several of those little Eastern states, ice that stops cross-continent traffic on Interstate 80 and coats transformers, pumps and trees with an inch and a half of glittering death.

" Right under the predictability of this flat country, drought, floods, industrial farming and genetically altered crops lie waiting to overturn lives and fortunes."

"I'll tell you, the book I want to read is called 'Nebraska'. A book with subtlety, one that describes surface calm while showing me that randomness lies in wait just beneath. One that acknowledges that in real life nothing is 'predictable'."

—September 2015

Like a terrier

I notice people approach problem-solving in about as many ways as there are people.

When my husband mulls over an issue, or thinks his way through a project, he fits the cliché "like a dog worrying a bone." Sometimes I think he chews that bone long after the juice has gone out of it.

Other people describe their problem-solving process as finding a thread and following it—the Hansel and Gretel idea. Others wait for their version of God or the universe to provide a solution. Writers sometimes use that deus ex machina solution.

A counselor tells me most people aren't introspective at all; they reflexively choose the easiest path that appears.

I see my approach as like a terrier who sees something sticking up from the ground and digs after it, only to discover, once she has found it—with her head still in the hole—that there's something more, just beyond reach.

So she digs on, and turns up an interlocking idea or piece of the puzzle, then other bits, until the supply peters out. The digger grabs what she can carry in her teeth, backs out and lies on the grass, brushing bits of dirt off her nose and surveys the parts of an idea or issue or problem she's excavated.

If they're not enough, she may make other trips into regions where insights lie, digging new holes to the left or right of the original. Eventually, scattered around her will lie components that she hopes will coalesce into a response, or answer, or a path ahead.

Even after all that work, sometimes those pieces of information or facts or insights don't add up, and the reluctant terrier lets the whole matter drop. Not every problem can be solved.

—2015

Men are such interesting creatures

A cursory glance as he headed for the driver's side prompted Jim to say, "Your car has a nail in the back left tire. Let's take mine."

Later we drove my car to the shop. The mechanic with the beautiful name elevated the rear, he and my husband leaned over together. Karob slowly turned the wheel, his hand sliding lightly over the dusty surface.

"There it is."

The men grinned in unison and relaxed.

Squinting in the sunshine I brought my face to within inches, finally I could see it, a tiny, shiny pinprick in dusty black rubber.

How on earth did that little thing attract Jim's attention? How come it appeared on the part of the tire where he could see it? I don't get how that happens.

—September 2013

Boys will be boys

The Northwest seemed exotic in ways, coming from the Great Plains as I did. I tried to understand it, bit by bit.

At the newspaper where I worked, the copy editor and one of the reporters roomed together on a houseboat moored on the Oregon side of the river.

How glamorous, I thought, to live on the water, to walk a gangplank to the front door. I pictured what I would do with such a location—the sleek Danish teak furniture, soft blues and browns, my Blenko glass to catch water reflections, deep sofas. I could almost feel the gentle sway as boats passed, hear the wind chime responding to breezes off the water.

Then one day they invited us to see this novel way of living.

I should have guessed. It looked like any other bachelor pad. Castoff furniture, brick and board bookshelves, beanbag chairs.

Took all the romance out of the idea of living on the water.

—1957

My relationship with people

Interesting trumps most other characteristics.

Observations for years

Mysterious, isn't it?

We choose some friends;
Some friends choose us.

Observations for years

Ode to cheap chocolate

Every year at Halloween, Snickers, Mars and Twix make their appearance in "fun" sizes. I've grown sophisticated enough to love single-sourced chocolate (the equivalent of single-malt Scotch). Yet every time I'm faced with two-bite packets of childhood I forget that.

—2016

On the prairies

The eyes of prairie people seek the horizon, and I am a prairie person.

Always

Perils of living in my mind, which often seems to be elsewhere

- "Turn here," he said, gesturing left. I did. Right into the path of an oncoming pickup truck. Car totaled; pickup okay; no one hurt.
- As I rounded the corner by my house, my grandmother's silver teapot, cream and sugar containers slid across the seat. I reached for them, neglecting to change wheel direction. Smashed into a neighbor's parked car. Silver service undamaged; no injuries.
- On the walking path in Kauai, a shuttle bus passed me moving faster than usual. Puzzled, I turned to watch it whiz past. I continued to walk on the edge between asphalt and grass

and forgot to watch my footing. I fell hard,
and broke my right arm.

—1954, 1954, 2007

Politically Correct

"Is it politically correct to call Mr. Bihn an oriental gardener?" Linda asked hesitantly. "It has a faintly, oh, I don't know, condescending sound."

The question surprised me.

When I wasn't paying attention, had Oriental become an offensive term? What about investment-grade Oriental rugs? Is something wrong with that? Yes, I know, "Asian" is replacing "Oriental" in contemporary use, but I thought that was just a change of fashion. Fashion changes often and English is fluid.

The uglier slang words no longer are in general use. In World War II usage "Jap" was intentionally dismissive; our current usage of "Japanese" conveys much more respect. Ah. That's the point of political correctness, isn't it? To convey respect? Is Oriental disrespectful?

With too many ideas swirling, I took refuge in facts. "Linda, his business card says, 'Mr. Bihn, Oriental Gardener.'"

—October 2005

Random thoughts on the way down the hall to take a nap

Artists call it negative space—the blank area between or around representations on canvas or film.

The words are not an opinion or a value judgment, as in negative = bad. They're a description: negative = nothing there.

Nothing means *no thing,* but how can this be when we can see it and name it? Space is *a* thing, not *no* thing, I think.

Art often needs space to enhance objects or people.

So do I.

I'm going to get some right here and now. I'm putting a nap (good ole negative space!) between me and my next activity.

—February 2007

Religion and McDonalds

Transubstantiation, prayer wheels, incense, scrolls, carbs, calories, low fat, high fat, no fat.

I've come to believe that religion and food programs, diets, eating systems, whatever you call them, have this similarity: in the end, you just pick the one that suits you.

Religions and diets purport to get you to the same place, whether it's called heaven, salvation, enlightenment, weight loss or health.

We all have backgrounds that lead us in a direction: the country we're born in, the prevailing culture, how our mothers cooked.

In spite of these backgrounds many of us end up elsewhere. Christians embrace Buddhism, Catholics leave the fold and follow an Indian mystic, agnostics convert to Judaism, Muslims become secular. Millions profess no "religion," but call themselves "spiritual." Happens every day, announced or not.

Vegetarians come from meat-and-potatoes families, raw food devotees from overcooked food households, and eat-your-organic-food kids turn to McDonalds.

In the name of reducing high blood pressure and cholesterol people choose Adkins' high protein, low carb methods or embrace DASH, a low fat, high fruit and vegetable system. They earnestly count at Weight Watchers, or count calories alone, aiming to control obesity, to become fit.

With both religion and food, converts have "reasons" for their choice and can recite them at length. But I've come to believe we just find something that suits us and develop a rationale to fit it.

—August 21, 2010

The wonder of it

I have small knack for fitting in, yet I am loved.

I wasn't given the gift of contentment, yet I am happy.

—2016

We have differing roles in life

My job is to help people figure out what they want to do and then help them to do it.

A lifetime of thinking about it

What? My child is an introvert?

Studies show that employees closely observe their bosses, know a lot about them, discuss them, work at understanding them. But bosses seldom do the same with employees. The assumption is that since bosses/managers/supervisors have power over employees, they loom as hugely important to the less powerful. Pleasing them, knowing their characteristics, is a survival technique

I wonder if the same is true of children and parents. I'll bet on average children study their parents, think about them, perhaps understand them, more than parents do children. I think many youngsters know their parents better than those parents know their children.

—September, 2015

Women alone

I've noticed, over the years, that my women friends who live alone, whether divorced, single or widowed, have an edge that most of my married friends do not.

My theory is that it's because the single ones are responsible for their own financial welfare, and perhaps that of children.

In the suburban, middle-class world I inhabit, men generally assume responsibility for those same things, and they have an edge, too. They seem more sure of what they will and will not do, more ready to make decisions by themselves. They seem more willing to say no and to make mistakes.

In spite of ourselves, married women of a certain age often eventually come to rely on the financial acumen of husbands, even if we contribute to the household bottom line. Even if finances become a shared responsibility.

I think this softens our ability to assume leadership, to think for ourselves, to make firm decisions. To be willing to be wrong.

True independence demands financial independence.

—2016

Thoughts about guilt

Guilt is like a letter delivered to your door: what you do with it is up to you. You can accept or reject it.

Here's how I deal with the issue, just in case it appeals to you.

First decide whether this guilt is yours, or someone else's. If another person is trying to make you feel guilty, and you're not, that's manipulation, best ignored.

However, if the guilt belongs to you, do something about it. Make a plan.

You can confront it: apologize, make amends, change behavior, resolve not to do whatever it was again, or dig into the guilt to see what can be learned from it. You can ignore it; not all battles must be fought.

There's no right or wrong for every case—each one must be decided separately. The plan's the thing:

Identify the feeling, name it, determine ownership, make a plan, do it, and move on. This will release guilt's hold, release energy for moving ahead.

Keeping and re-reading the guilt letter does no good.

—1996

Why?

Did I intend to? No.

Did I want to? Not really.

Did I do it? Yes.

Such is every life…a mix of intention and happenstance.

—January 2017

In general, I like to keep my miniatures light. The world is full enough of black and dark gray, dissonance and difficulty without me adding to it. I want to offer you just some little thing to think about, swift shafts of light to the darkness. I don't fancy dark will go away, but maybe I can diffuse it a little.

Even so, some thoughts are "closer to the bone," as the poet says. Here are a few.

Adrienne Rich

First Congregational Church downtown Portland. Filled.

She's four years older than I, this angry revolutionary. What looks like rheumatoid arthritis has put her in a wheeled walker. She inches to us from the wings slowly, deliberately, in the manner of people who hurt.

She's introduced as Ahhhdrienne, an exhaled breath softening the "a," as our teacher Ana pronounces hers. Maybe it's a poet thing, the soft, breathed "a."

"This is the first reading I've given sitting down," she begins.

Aging revolutionary, yes, but the poems remain strong and fearless. More revolutionary than aging, I think. Still angry. An icon for those of a certain time.

Can icons be tiny and frail? Mother Teresa was, wasn't she?

—Portland, Oregon, March 20, 2006

Before he was Nathaniel

Before he took back his birth name of Nathaniel, before he called himself Nathan, I knew him as Nate.

His first teaching gig was at the University of Nebraska, the beginning of a long career of teaching, mentoring, and drinking beer with students. Ken Rystrom, my fiance, and I babysat his first daughter before we were graduated. We knew his family, followed his career, and stayed in touch.

Love at first sight

Our three daughters knew Nate, and he captivated their children. Eventually I journeyed to the shores of Blackfoot Lake in Montana to introduce my new husband to him.

When we first met, my audacity appealed to Nate. I told him (and the Publications Board) I'd had such good journalism training in high school that I could work immediately for the University student newspaper without taking his introduction to journalism class. My boldness carried the day and Nate let me enroll in his second year class while I began reporting for the Daily Nebraskan, a powerful influence in my life and career.

Audacity not only appealed to him, but it applied to him. He was a conspiracy theorist and boldly claimed the title, often with a cheeky grin. He loved tweaking authority.

He claimed not to recognize that he was the sexiest man in any gathering, but I told him I never believed it.

Nate Blumberg, 1922-2012

—2012

By the numbers

The daughter who doesn't ask for help, asks for help. Her husband filed for divorce and notified her by email.

We respond.

Two flights get us to Memphis.

We rent a sixteen-foot yellow Penske truck.

Two days and four friends help load it.

Three chickens are given away, including the silly one with a topknot that looks like Phyllis Diller.

For seventeen hundred miles and three nights we caravan across four states.

Three friends appear in Colorado. At eighty-six hundred feet, we and they empty the truck in two hours, shoehorning chairs, a futon, bookcases, computers and dishes from a thirty-five hundred square foot house into a thousand square foot rental.

What number should be assigned to a daughter's bruised heart?

—September 7, 2009

Being loveable

The rambunctious, larger-than-life Bohemian men, my uncles, and the complex, colorful women who married them—and stayed married to them—seemed not to be concerned about being loveable.

If they thought about it at all, and I doubt they did, perhaps they'd have said other parts of life occupied them: being successful, having fun, doing and saying what they thought was right, being true to themselves, being of service to their communities and helping people who crossed their paths.

They weren't loveable, these uncles and aunts. Many of them were formidable, loud, domineering, and opinionated in an "I don't care who agrees" way. A few of their personalities exuded warmth, although not all.

The men had a sentimental side…they would cry without shame and they could laugh until they cried. I don't think the aunts were sentimental.

The world had to take them all into account, had to deal with colorful personalities and strong characters. They earned the world's respect, too: the medical doctor, the lawyer and the banker, the teacher and the nurse, early women college graduates, a thespian.

Growing up among them taught me that "interesting" trumps "likeable," "being congruent" beats out "loveable."

I'm still drawn to people like them.

My friends are a stimulating lot.

—November, 2000

Old love: a status report*

My first love—we called it "boyfriend" then—lies dying in a faraway town we once shared. His wife sends emails. Participating in the distant drama through the electronic web woven when we click "forward," many former classmates wait with her.

She reports the grip he holds on life, his refusal to let go, coupled with his inability to speak, much less rally. He is caught in a slow process, but he's battled it to a standstill. He and death are even-steven for a while.

She says he weeps. I believe it's not from sorrow but in frustration at not being able to improve. The person I knew would regard dying as the next step and not fear it. But he's accustomed to winning.

I read the updates from across the country and admire this man for not relinquishing his tenacity, his strength and willingness to do battle with the odds.

Before we left high school, he became one of the last Americans to contract polio, and he battled it then as he battles now, with a handsome body and a strong will. The inspiration of his fight sent him on to medical school, then back to practice in our hometown.

Unknown to us all, the polio lurked. Fifty years after we thought he'd conquered the disease its aftereffects found him. As in this current struggle, he'd pulled off a stalemate but the outcome was not in doubt.

But to him belongs the good fight, and I salute him.

—Winter, 2009

**I think the idea "old love" came from a prompt.*

Immortality

The idea of immortality, of leaving something to carry on where you left off—the family name, a book, a building, a business—is a male idea. It's less important for many women because they have immortality built in. Children are their immortality. A child's imprint is first and foremost that of the mother—and that imprint carries on, good or bad, whether you like it or not.

Some men never know whether they're being continued in the world through another human being. Others don't care. Or don't see a child as a permanent link through generations.

So they need to leave something else behind. Something less fluid or erratic or less subject to outside influences than a person. Something they can control—a pyramid, a statue, a home by the river.

Some days I believe that. On others, I get realistic: not all women have children; not all men lust for immortality.

—February 2009

Impending change

I've been conscious of it since my last birthday. Moving from autumn into winter, through spring, summer and now autumn again. Every day during this year I am the age of my mother when she died.

Flashes of this uneasy knowledge visit me steadily. I don't know why, can't imagine that I'm so conscious of it.

Will the malaise disappear when I awake into the year that means I've outlived her? On the day I am older than she ever was will I emerge a fresh creature like an old butterfly that struggles out of its worn chrysalis?

Or will my uneasiness dissipate slowly as I move into this newness, as one always does?

—April 19, 2009

The year I became obsolete

I chose to become invisible to the world of work when I retired, no longer making myself known in the halls of commerce. But on the domestic front I thought I had a permanent position in the center of a world that, after all, was largely my creation. I relished my place as matriarch of this expanding universe.

My three daughters and the stepdaughter who is not-mine-yet-mine, have become suns in their own solar systems. They are orbited by children, husbands and dogs, complex jobs, writing projects, returning-to-school and the first grandchild.

The grandchildren are beginning to generate their own solar systems, surrounded by boyfriends, girlfriends, sports and where-to-go-to college. The oldest has a wife and brand new son.

I was surprised when the young mother intercepted my journey to the table, handing me her baby and his bottle.

Looking for a place to feed the week-old infant, I found myself sitting on a sofa across the room from the crowd around the Christmas table. From what seemed like a real distance, I watched them become louder and more festive, carving meat and passing champagne.

I think I should have enjoyed the promise of another eventual solar system lying content in my arms. But I didn't. I felt irrelevant and thought I could see my future, moving on without me.

—Christmas 2006

Your side

Forget the bedrock of shared values, the hammered out difficulties of those first six months of marriage when we fought daily. Forget the long years of shared pleas: "I'd really like to have you go with me."

Forget that my children have become yours, and yours, mine, that we know each other's friends, that people we held dear have died and we've cried over them together. Cried separately, for that matter.

We've laughed a lot, too, haven't we? With and at each other—between us all is forgiven in a giggle.

Forget all that. This is how I know it will last: When you're out of town, I sleep on your side of the bed, use your pillow, inhale your warm odor all night, every night, until you return.

Once a season

It comes once a season, always unexpectedly.

Perhaps candlelight reflecting from polished wood jostles a memory. Maybe the soprano sounds of a choir float—just so—into the heights and back again, landing in the spot in my heart where music triggers tears.

Today it came in my morning newspaper. A wreath-maker in Maine and his volunteer crews for years have been driving fresh green wreaths with red bows to Arlington cemetery in Washington, D.C., placing them one by one against the white, straight-rowed headstones.

A photo, all green and red and white, caught a slender young woman in jeans kneeling by a wreath-marked stone. Ranks of other markers ranged into the distance behind her, reminders of how big Arlington is. I thought of our local Willamette national cemetery where Paul's father lies, remembered cemeteries in Honolulu and Normandy.

A second photo showed streams of motorcycles, driven by more volunteers, escorting the wreath-trucks down the coast highway from Maine to D.C., and that did it. A piercing, sudden ache brought tears and I had to stop eating to wipe them away, there were so many.

So many tears, so many young men. We are killing them again, now, today. Ours and theirs. After this war is over, other wars in other places will destroy other mothers' sons. People do this to each other.

Even before decorations were unwrapped and the aroma of evergreens filled the house this year the unutterable, stabbing sadness of Christmas caught me by surprise.

—November 14, 2006

An accounting

On bad days I can chronicle ways the world has affected me, but I can't tell whether I have affected the world—and I wanted to. On those days I am filled with an underlying sadness to be one in the nameless, faceless masses of humans destined to disappear without a trace.

On good days, I feel I did pretty well with the hand I was dealt. I've taken my place in line, naïve and yearning, but head mostly up and shoulders squared. I've improved as the years passed.

I'm too realistic to be happy, but satisfied with much.

Found

I found these lines jotted in notes from a writing class. Did I copy them from a poem or essay? Are they mine? They could be.

She was less than she wanted to be
More than she might have been.

Acknowledgements

So many people help, knowingly or not, when a writer pulls a lifetime of experiences into essays like these. Cousin Jim Misko who writes fiction, one book right after the other, with ferocious concentration, gives me an example of how it's done in real time. Allan May and Gerry Bertsch, two poets; Gerry's astute wife Cynthia; Bob Buckley, engineer-lawyer; Jody Everts, painter, and Pam Gross, author and job-hunting specialist, read and commented, gave me a boost at various points when I needed it.

Every couple of months, a small group of writers meet for mutual support (Kim Cook, Martha Ragland, Jim Petersen, Suzanne Graham), and about as often another group meets to write together for a day (Kathleen Haley, Linda Chaplik, Ana Ramana, et al). These keep me going. As do the periodic questions about my work that come from four daughters and a great cadre of growing-up grands.

The painting on the cover is the work of Jody Everts; Anita Jones put it into a cover and formatted the book.

My final acknowledgement goes to my writer-spouse Jim, whose combination of support and pushy encouragement helps keep me afloat. Without you, I probably would fade into the sunset just sitting and playing solitaire on my iPhone.

Thank you all!

About the author

Sally Petersen's work has been in print through a career that spans journalism, essay writing, memoir, and running a writing, editing and desktop publishing business. She has been a food columnist and a life-planning consultant.

Her first book-length piece was non-fiction, about running a one-person business. Her second and third are collections of what she calls "miniatures," short essays, observations, stories, musings.

After most of a lifetime in the Pacific Northwest, she still thinks of herself as a Nebraskan, a Great Plains dweller surrounded by far horizons and unseen complexity. She and her husband Jim, also a writer, live near Portland, Oregon.

She adores her four daughters and every one of their children, fascinating and surprising as they are. Watching them differentiate themselves and find their vocations remains one of her favorite activities.

For more information, to buy additional books, or to contact Sally (she'd love to know your reactions to her work), go to her website, sallypetersen.com.